SAUNDARYA LAHARI

'Mani Rao's translations have a hard-won simplicity and ripeness. This joyful rendition of an iconic text will offer its share of literary delight, as well as a key to a deeper alchemy. These translations with their ease and lightness of touch will resonate with lovers of poetry as well as travellers on the path of the Divine Feminine.'

—ARUNDHATHI SUBRAMANIAM, author of *When God Is a Traveller*

SAUNDARYA LAHARI

WAVE OF BEAUTY

TRANSLATED FROM THE SANSKRIT BY

MANI RAO

HarperCollins *Publishers* India

First published in India by HarperCollins *Publishers* 2022
4th Floor, Tower A, Building No. 10, Phase II, DLF Cyber City,
Gurugram, Haryana – 122002
www.harpercollins.co.in

2 4 6 8 10 9 7 5 3 1

P-ISBN: 978-93-5629-234-5
E-ISBN: 978-93-5629-286-4

Image of the Śrīyantra in the book, courtesy: sunnychicka,
Alamy Stock Vector

Typeset in 10.5/14 Times New Roman at
Manipal Technologies Limited, Manipal

Printed and bound at
Thomson Press (India) Ltd

Satyam, Śivam, Sundaram

CONTENTS

SANSKRIT PRONUNCIATION

Sanskrit is a phonetically precise language. A letter can only be pronounced one way (whereas in English, a letter may have different pronunciations in different words). If you know how to pronounce the Sanskrit alphabet, you can read the language accurately. The chart below will help readers who may not know Sanskrit to pronounce the hymn correctly.

Sanskrit words, including names of gods and ancient commentators, are in Roman script with diacritical marks. (Thus, Ādi Śaṅkarācārya, but not Maṇi Rao or Tapasyānanda.) A dash over a vowel makes it a longer syllable. Curl your tongue back when there is a dot under the letter, except for 'ṃ', 'ḥ' and 'ṛ'. An 'h' after consonants calls for aspiration, or an out-breath, and so on.

Vowels:

a as in u in cut
ā as in father
i as in bit
ī as in beet
u as in put or foot
ū as in brute or cool
e as in bay or fate
ai as in sigh or aisle
o as in hope
au as in sound or flautist
ṛ (which is a vowel in Sanskrit) similar to brunch, or rig
ṃ where the preceding vowel is nasalized, so oṃ as in the French bon
ḥ softly echoes the preceding vowel

Consonants: as for English except for

v as in wall

ś as in shame (whereas s as in so)

ṣ similar to dish

c as in church or chutney

t as in pasta

ṅ as in sung

ñ as in canyon

ṇ has no equivalent in English, but it is a retroflex, i.e., the tongue needs to curl backwards to touch the palate and then hit the back of the teeth.

d as in the

ḍ as in dart

kh, gh, ch, jh, th, dh, ph, bh are aspirated consonants, i.e., the h is pronounced along with an out-breath. This sound has no exact equivalent in English, but the following examples will help approximate the sound. Thus, k as in skate but kh similar to Khan; g as in gate but gh as in the country, Ghana; ch as in much; and so on.

INTRODUCTION

Like an old chest kept in the corner of a room, an heirloom that is part of our heritage and that we often even sit upon but have never opened—sometimes a song or a poem can be familiar, and yet elusive. The Sanskrit hymn, *Saundarya Laharī,* is one such composition. Even though albums by leading voices in Carnatic music have made it a part of the Indian music landscape, and there are numerous audio and even video renditions of it online, the title 'Saundarya Laharī' is not immediately recognizable, even in India. 'Saundarya' means beauty, and 'laharī' is that which has a wave, and this may be why some interpret the word as 'flood', 'tide', or even 'ocean'. Oceans are recurring symbols in Indian mythology and conceal treasures which can only be obtained through the exertion of special effort.

Saundarya Laharī praises goddess Śakti as the ultimate divine power. The word 'Śakti' means 'power' in common parlance; as a name of the goddess, it connotes her absolute power over the universe. Śakti is considered feminine energy and is paired with Śiva, who embodies masculine energy. Whereas Śiva represents consciousness, Śakti represents the creative force in the universe, the kinetic energy that activates and animates consciousness. Only Śakti's vibrations (spandanas) cause the universe to be generated and set in motion. As the Devī Bhāgavata Purāṇa puts it, Śiva is śava (corpse) without Śakti. In *Saundarya Laharī*, the vibrant, pulsing force of Śakti is felt as waves, sometimes light and sometimes pounding.

BASIC CONCEPTS

A brief outline will be helpful to those unfamiliar with Indian mythology and the basic concepts of tantric traditions. In legends and epic histories (itihāsa-purāṇas), the gods (surās) live in heaven (svarga), and there are three main figures—Brahmā (who creates), Viṣṇu (who preserves) and Śiva (who annihilates, or transforms). These three gods have spouses—Śiva's spouse is Pārvatī, the daughter of Himavān (the lord of the Himalaya mountains), Brahmā's is Sarasvatī (goddess of learning), and Viṣṇu's is Lakṣmī (the goddess of wealth). Pārvatī's alter ego is goddess Śakti.

Gods are honoured with religious rituals and hymns that praise them and describe their stories. They play a vital role in the running of the universe, and they support as well as hinder human affairs. The attitude of human beings towards gods is typically that of devotion (bhakti), entreaties and surrender. Intense devotion may also give rise to a sense of intimacy and imagining a god as one's beloved. Sacred utterances regarded as visionary revelations (mantras) and ritual procedures form the backbone of two (arguably) distinct strands of oral texts and ritual practices called 'veda' and 'tantra'. Among these, tantrism places the dyad of Śiva and Śakti at the centre.

Śiva and Śakti are considered immanent and present in every person. Śakti is described as present at the base of the spine in our body and is called kuṇḍalini. Cakras are like energy centres in our body along the path of the spine; we have seven cakras: mūlādhāra (base of spine), svādhiṣṭhāna (lower abdomen), maṇipūra (upper abdomen), anāhata (heart), viśuddha (throat), ājñā (eyebrows) and sahasrāra (crown). Treatises on and practitioners of yoga assert that kuṇḍalini Śakti coils three and a half times, like a serpent, at the base of the spine. Spiritual practice (sādhanā), ritual worship, and devotional absorption into the idea and form of Śakti cause kuṇḍalini Śakti to stir and rise along the cakras to the sahasrāra where it/she 'unites' with Śiva, or consciousness, causing a blissful experience (satcidānanda), as well as an awakening that is dubbed self-realization. Such an experience is believed to release a person from the repetitive cycle of birth and death (saṁsāra), and is therefore called liberation (mokṣa).

A more approachable name for Śakti is simply 'goddess' or 'Devī', and that is how *Saundarya Laharī* often refers to her. In tantra, even though the adoration appears to an outsider like duality (dvaita), the process and result are actually that of identification. Tantric worship begins by annihilating oneself and installing the divine within oneself—

thus identified, one can worship the divine, which is one's true self. The physical body is no enemy to the spirit; on the contrary, it is the expression of the self, and the medium that allows us to realize our self as transcendent. In fact, the 'body' may be understood better as a vehicle, device or instrument (yantra), rather than as physical matter. As yantra, then, the body is also made of mantra, and mantra mediates our access to its inner space. Sādhakas (seekers or practitioners) are usually initiated in mantras by a guru (teacher) who has the spiritual credentials to impart that mantra. Every verse of *Saundarya Laharī* is considered a mantra.

ŚRĪVIDYĀ TANTRA

The particular form of Śakti/Devī that *Saundarya Laharī* invokes is a benign goddess by the name of Tripura Sundarī (the beauty of three cities), one who is associated with a system called Śrīvidyā or Śrīcakra.

In addition to her iconic form, Śakti takes the form of a diagram made primarily of triangles and called a cakra (circuit, wheel) or yantra (diagram, device). In the ritual, the worshipper's contemplation moves from the outer perimeter of the cakra to the centre. Śakti also takes a verbal form, a tripartite sixteen-syllable vidyā (knowledge) or mantra (mystic utterance). In the preparatory stages, the sādhaka mentally desiccates, burns and inundates her/his own body and reconstructs a body made of syllables, thus becoming fit to identify with Śakti in the ritual.

The Śrīvidyā mantra of syllables and the Śrīcakra yantra of sequential circuits are part of an intricate cosmology. Language is at the heart of the concept. The creative energy of Śakti becomes a bindu (the dot at the centre of the cakra) of phonic energy and gives rise to a matrix of phonemes (mātṛkās), which in turn results in the world of objects and meanings. Contemplating and uttering the mantra, the worshipper makes offerings to the cakra. The Śrīvidyā tradition has a legacy of numerous texts on metaphysics and cosmology, and manuals on ritual methodology. The actual ritual of Śrīvidyā is esoteric—it is said that the sixteenth syllable of the mantra is regarded as so secret, even a teacher initiating a student may only write it on sand and then erase it at once. *Saundarya Laharī* is considered an important source for the study and practice of Śrīvidyā.

SEX AND POLITICS

Devī's position is higher than all deities, and several verses in *Saundarya Laharī* illustrate this point dramatically. The three main gods, Brahmā, Viṣṇu and Śiva, and the chief of the gods, Indra, are all subservient to her. Verses describe them worshipping the dust from Devī's feet (2), standing in wait beside her feet, bowing (22, 25 and 29), or waiting at her door (95). Devī's husband Śiva is intensely jealous of the aśoka tree that she kicks (see note on verse 85) and in the very next verse, she kicks his forehead because he falters on her name. But the emphasis on the subservience of the male gods cannot be taken at face value. We cannot but help wince at the sharp contrast to our world, where women lack opportunities and their own Śakti is blatantly oppressed. The hymn then seems a cruel joke, or perhaps an obverse indication of social reality, and one wonders if it is because women are in an inferior position socially that the position of the feminine divine has to be described in such an exaggerated manner. Secondly, Devī's family status is underlined—she is addressed mostly as the daughter of the mountain, or as the consort/wife of Śiva. Descriptions of her physical features rely often on dramatizations of her role as daughter and wife—her chin is stroked by her father, and is kissed by, even *fit* to be grasped by, her husband (67), and she has pretty knees because she kneels down to her husband (82). Her spousal fidelity becomes a point of commendation—her inaccessibility is attributed to her fidelity (96), and compared to Sarasvatī (Brahmā's spouse) and Lakṣmī (Viṣṇu's spouse) whose favours are easier to garner.

The world of *Saundarya Laharī* is heteronormative. In verse 12, the poet declares Devī more beautiful than the celestial beauties Rambhā and Urvaśī; these demi-goddesses are so impressed by Devī's unapproachable beauty that they wish to be one with Śiva just so they can be closer to Devī. Even as the poet positions Devī as the ultimate power, his own voice and imagination are rooted in the idea of male domination (96). Verse 18 says that meditating on the red-hued form of Devī will make the devotee capable of captivating even celestial courtesans. On the one hand, the poet of *Saundarya Laharī* claims the highest position for Devī, a female divine; but at the same time, his own power is expressed by the subjugation of women, even celestial women. How then may women devotees of Devī relate to such a scheme?

Typically, in Indian narratives, we find an overarching tension between the indulgence of erotic desires and an ideal of self-control. However, in tantric sources, the aesthetic and erotic are creative, and lead to bliss. *Saundarya Laharī*'s descriptions of Devī's physical features are exuberant and candid. Some commentators refrain from translating verses 72 to 83 and even note that dwelling upon Devī's physical beauty may trigger inappropriate thoughts; such anxieties are not to be found in the hymn itself. From a spiritual perspective, imagining the physical form is only a method for one-pointed focus and absorption.

For a reader, there are ways to overcome the discomfiture from the tone of misogyny or apparent eroticism in *Saundarya Laharī*. In my view, even revelations (śrutis) are ultimately collaborative—seers may receive inspiration from beyond but can only transmit that in the medium of their own voice, which necessarily belongs to a social-historical context and also has its own unique personality. We may also consider *Saundarya Laharī* in the context of the philosophical underpinnings of the tantric system. As the female principle, Śakti is not limited to women—she is present in all people, and all devotees including male devotees strive to identify with her. Seen this way, *Saundarya Laharī* cannot be about one-upmanship (or one-upwomanship). It emphasizes that Śiva and Śakti are one, they are inseparable. The union of Śakti and Śiva is about the unity of self, and the sublime bliss of liberation. Finally, all objections based on meaning are banished the moment you experience the effects of *Saundarya Laharī*'s mantras.

LEVELS OF MEANING

Engaging with *Saundarya Laharī* takes one into its expansive world. At the basic level, there are references to legends from the purāṇas (ancient stories, including stories of the gods), descriptions of the diagrammatic form and enclosures of the Śrīyantra, and to the cakras of the body. Such associative meanings are relatively easy to learn. Sometimes, the interpretive possibilities are many; a simple example—there are a number of options about just who might be referenced by the word 'ādi' in the very first verse, a word which literally means 'et cetera'.

Additionally, the imagery of *Saundarya Laharī* points to an otherworldly realm—for instance, the verse that describes the dwelling place of the goddess as a gem-encrusted island surrounded by celestial or wish-fulfilling trees (8). Either we make this fantastic realm a part of our imagination, or we consider it symbolic and seek guidance from tantric sources and erudite commentators. The imagery in verse 8 is also mentioned in numerous tantric sources. The *Lalitāsahasranāmam* (the thousand names of Lalitā) describes the house made of wish-fulfilling gemstones 'cintāmaṇigṛhāntasthā'; the *Rājarājeśvarī Tantra* describes the island of 'Maṇidvīpa' in the ocean of nectar, while also giving measurements of this ocean; the *Bhairavayāmala Tantra* describes the seat of the goddess, where the four legs or posts are Brahmā, Viṣṇu, Rudra and Īśvara, and the seat is Sadāśiva himself.

Beyond the associative and the symbolic, there are the esoteric meanings. *Saundarya Laharī* is considered a mālā mantra (garland mantra)—each verse is a distinct mantra. A mantra is a naturally occurring sound form or formula, discovered or intuited by a poet or seer at a moment of extraordinary insight. In turn, it can be deployed by the person who articulates the mantra or arrives at some competence over the mantra for specific results. Famously, verses/mantras 15, 16 and 17 are said to confer the devotee with poetic talent, and verses/mantras 18 and 19, with the power to attract women (good luck).

Beyond the mantras and their magical properties, there are hidden or coded aspects—it is widely believed that *Saundarya Laharī* is actually in 'saṃdhyā bhāṣā' (twilight language). The sixteen words in the first half of the first verse have been thought to refer to the sixteen-syllable mantra. Some mantras are thought to point to other mantras. According to commentator Kaivalyāśrama, the very first verse/mantra indicates the mantras 'prasāda', 'anuttarā', 'mātṛkā', 'vāgvādinī', 'śaivapañcākśarī' and 'pāśāḍi-traiākśarī'. As a part of tantra, each mantra goes along with a 'prayoga' (ritual application). The first mantra must be recited 1,000 times for twelve days, with a particular yantra drawn on a gold plate in which the bījākśara (root syllable) of 'klīṃ' is inscribed. (This will result in success for any and every task.)

Any reader who wishes to go to such depth, whether to understand the history of ideas and responses to the verse or to follow the ritual uses of the mantra, would do well to make this book only a starting point and then to explore the commentaries—there are over thirty-five in Sanskrit alone, and many in other Indian languages. My suggestion is to enter the world of *Saundarya Laharī*, read the meanings, articulate the mantras, and memorize them if you can. Let the meanings and the sound resonate in your body and mind, be overcome and humbled by the beauty and power of Śakti, and beseech her that you may experience the beauty and bliss of *Saundarya Laharī*.

IT'S A POEM

There are 100 verses in *Saundarya Laharī*, although some versions have up to 103 verses. The first part of forty-one verses called 'Ānanda Laharī' (Wave of Bliss) describes Devī's power, her manifestations, and her embodied presence within the devotee. The second part is called 'Saundarya Laharī' (Wave of Beauty). Verses 42-91 describe Devī's physical beauty, moving from head to toe. Verses 92 onwards are more akin to prayers.

Saundarya Laharī is composed in quatrains, in śikhariṇī metre, which is a syllabic metre of seventeen syllables in each quarter (pāda). For a line to be in śikhariṇī, its second, third, fourth, fifth, sixth, twelfth, thirteenth and seventeenth syllables must be 'guru' (heavy/long) while the rest of the syllables are 'laghu' (short/light). (Sanskrit has guru and laghu syllables, unlike English which has long and short syllables, and there are specific rules for identifying them.)[1]

Apart from metrical dexterity, even the sounds within the line play off each other—for instance, 'truṭita-taṭinī' (79), 'sadyaḥ svidya' (80). Often, there is an exploration of the range of derived words in a single verse—for instance, 'padaṃ', 'prapadaṃ', 'apadaṃ' and 'vipadāṃ' (88). Sometimes, a word is used in its various meanings—for instance, verse 61 uses the word 'vaṃśa' for three of its meanings: nose-ridge, bamboo staff and lineage.

The hymn feels personal and even intimate; it is addressed directly to Devī, and most verses include the vocative case (such as O Devī). Devī is addressed by any of her many names—Devī, Pārvatī, Śivé (consort of Śiva), Śambhoḥ (Śiva's), Śarvāṇī (Śarva's, i.e., Śiva's spouse) and often as jananī (mother) and giri-tanayā (daughter of the mountain). The Sanskrit word for 'goddess' is 'Devī', and that is how I refer to her in the translation and notes.

Words seem to have been chosen extremely carefully in this hymn, and the choice of Devī's name is a good example. For instance, in verse 81, Devī is called by her name 'Pārvatī', a word that is derived from 'parvata' which means 'mountain'. Devī's father is Himavān, and his name in this verse, 'kṣitidharapati', literally means 'bearer of the earth'. This provides a delightful contrast to the central idea of the verse, that Pārvatī's hips are bigger than the earth, and make the earth light by comparison. However, in verse 60, Devī is called 'Śarvāṇī', and the appellation precedes the word 'śravaṇa'; we know it is not a coincidence and can marvel at the skill of the poet.

Many of the comparisons in the hymn follow conventions of Sanskrit aesthetics. The natural world provides the scope—thus, faces and feet are compared to lotuses, glances to arrows, breasts to the temples of elephants, thighs to plantain stems, and so on. Correlations often occur due to numbers. Devī has four hands, and Brahmā has four heads that hope for the protective blessing from her four hands (70). The two earrings of Devī reflected on her cheeks become four, and provide a basis for comparison with the four wheels of a chariot.

The description of Devī's beauty is done by means of elaborate tropes and comparisons. A few examples will help illustrate this point, especially verse 44 where the expression 'saundarya laharī' (wave of beauty) occurs. The ocean of beauty of Devī's face is so vibrant that the waves spill over into her hair-parting where she wears a vermilion mark (sindūra). Flanked by thick hair, the parting reminds the poet of sunrise upon the no man's land between two thronging armies. If the comparison is a stretch, it points to the transcendence of Devī's beauty and illustrates the inadequacy of both language and imagination for the task of description. In verse 45, the poet says that Devī's face is so lovely that it mocks a lotus, and illustrates it by comparing her soft curls to the loveliness of a swarm of baby bees. Śiva's eyes—the same eyes that razed Kāma to the ground—are like bees, maddened or intoxicated by the beauty of Devī's face. The poet uses another word for the bee-like eyes of Śiva—'honey-licker'—which lets Devī's face be automatically compared to a honey-laden flower, as well as Śiva's eyes to an intoxicated bee. A connection is made between the state of being mad with anger and mad with attraction. The detail that her curly hair is like a swarm of *young* bees suggests textural softness as well as movement and density.

SOURCES AND VERSIONS

It is widely believed that the author of *Saundarya Laharī*—or at least the first part of *Saundarya Laharī*—is Ādi Śaṅkarācārya (Śaṅkara), the seer from Kerala who wrote the commentary for the Brahmāsūtra, established religious centres across the Indian region and is believed to have lived around the eighth century CE. Sanskrit commentaries pay reverential homage to Śaṅkara in the very first line. There are legends about how Śaṅkara brought back the first forty-one verses called 'Ānanda Laharī' from Kailāśa, i.e., Śiva's abode in the Himalayas. In verse 75, the poet calls himself a child of Draviḍa (Draviḍa śiśu)—scholars have speculated about the reference, wondering if it refers to some South Indian poet other than Śaṅkara. There seems to be some hesitation among commentators attributing the second part of the hymn, which describes Devī's beautiful body, to the celibate monk Śaṅkara. Whether this reasoning is flawed or not, the authorship cannot be proved. What we can say with certainty is that the squeamishness says more about the interpreters than about the interpreted.

Locating *Saundarya Laharī* in around the eighth century CE would align with the rich imagery and profusion of aesthetic emotions (*rasas*), by then so practised and perfected by Sanskrit poets, especially Kālidāsa. But establishing dates is like walking on a minefield, potent with explosive arguments, and authenticity is an impossible or naïve pursuit considering the oral transmission of *Saundarya Laharī* over centuries. There are thirty-five Sanskrit commentaries of *Saundarya*

Laharī, and well known among these are the ones by Lakṣmīdhara, Kaivalyāśrama (called *Saubhāgyavardhanī*), Kāmeśvara Sūri (called *Aruṇāmodinī*), Ānandagirī, Rāmakavi (called *Ḍiṇḍima Bhāṣya*) and Gopālasundarī. Sanskrit is not the only literature of discussion for *Saundarya Laharī*, and there are numerous books in Tamil, Telugu and other Indian languages. During my fieldwork in Andhra–Telangana, I found several contemporary scholars of religion who had print and audio publications in Telugu. Many Hindu institutions, such as the Sringeri Peetham, publish discourses on *Saundarya Laharī*. Even when authors state that they have adhered to Lakṣmīdhara's commentary, very few mention details about the manuscripts to which they have referred. The order of verses varies slightly between versions, and there are even alternative versions for words in many verses resulting in variant meanings. One can only appreciate uncertainty and multiplicity as a part of the delightful or just inevitable legacy of an oral tradition.[2]

I was able to peruse numerous palm-leaf and paper manuscripts at the Adyar Library in Chennai. These were in Telugu, Kannada, Malayalam, Odiya and Nagari scripts, and did not carry any information about the dates or sources. The library digitized four folios that I selected, in Telugu and Nagari, among which only one was complete. PM-77456 had nine verses, and PM-73056 had seventeen verses, both in Telugu. The Nagari manuscript PM-2918 had 103 verses, and PM-2917 was fragmentary with marginal commentary on each folio. The Mysore edition reproduced in Vol. 11 of the *Bibiliotheca Sanskrita* of the Government Oriental Library Series by the Government of Mysore is the acknowledged source for Swami Tapasyananda (1987), Pandit S. Subrahmanya Sastri and T.R. Srinivasa Ayyangar (1965) and A. Kuppuswami (1976). All three follow the same order for the first forty-one verses, i.e., 'Ānanda Laharī'. Here, the twenty-eighth verse is 'dadāne karatalai…', a verse which is placed as the ninetieth or ninety-first in some versions. I too follow this sequence.

ON THIS TRANSLATION

Many practitioners adhere to the idea that mantras are sounds, effective in themselves, and meanings only help intentionality and focus. Of course, the original Sanskrit is reproduced in this book, both in Roman script with diacritical marks and in the Nagari script. However, meaning is also an easy point of entry and can whet the appetite of those who are not yet aficionados of *Saundarya Laharī*.

This translation is not a guidebook for religious rituals. Ritual observances with *Saundarya Laharī* involve the use of yantras and bīja mantras (seed syllables). Some commentators derive mantras from each verse and stipulate yantras and rituals for each verse together with the goals or results. Tantric rituals are typically a part of an overall sādhanā, involve initiation (dīkṣā) and call for some personal disciplines; I would caution the reader not to experiment with rituals without a guide or guru. My translation aims to broaden the reach of this spectacular hymn, and let curious readers experience some of its beauty in translation.

I was first attracted to *Saundarya Laharī* in 2010. An early version of my translation of the first seventeen verses was published in *Asymptote* (2010)—thank you *Asymptote* editors, for this initial encouragement and readership. Then, my work came to an abrupt halt and I felt unable to proceed further; perhaps I felt disallowed, or just unready. During my doctoral research into mantra in tantric communities, *Saundarya Laharī* kept tapping my shoulder. At Devipuram, I met a sādhaka by the name of Sheela who shared astonishing experiences of promptings and visitations by Kālī (a form of Devī) after she began to study *Saundarya Laharī*.[3] In Iowa City, Usha Balakrishnan shared mind-boggling narratives of how she would heal ailments by singing specific verses from *Saundarya Laharī* over the phone. But it was ten years from when I first began to translate the hymn that I actually felt not equipped to the task. I cannot thank Urvashi Butalia enough, whose periodic nudges helped keep the project firmly on my to-do list over that entire time.

During the challenging years of 2020 and 2021, I found myself turning to sādhanā. As I 'read'—or did—*Saundarya Laharī*, I felt its mantras reverberating within my body, and found that it sensitized me to my own vibrations. Reading led to translation. Devoting time and attention to each verse/mantra was a way to absorb their sounds, meanings and associations, and to be open to their effects. As I translated each mantra, I would also try to memorize it. After that, understanding the meaning involved first the padayojanā (prose order), understanding the relationships between the parts of the verse, and then referring to dictionaries and commentaries. And yet, very often, the real heart of the verses felt untouched. The uplifting moments were during sādhanā, when an experience was recognizable as something that had been described in *Saundarya Laharī*.

But even sādhanā is only successful when supported by the universe. Karuna Sivasailam's own study of *Saundarya Laharī* occurred at the same time as my renewed engagement with it, and her crystalline voice often played in my mind's ear—hence, performing this hymn and translation together has been gratifying. A big hug to Shinie Antony, whose astute appraisal I value greatly, and who placed this book with HarperCollins. My heartfelt thanks to Rahul Soni, for his brilliant editorial direction, and the strong team at HarperCollins, especially Rinita Banerjee. Thank you to the staff at the Adyar Library in Chennai, who made my trip fruitful despite travel restrictions. I am indebted to all the great writers and translators of the past and present who have worked with *Saundarya Laharī*. Finally, to the boss, Bhavāni tvaṃ…

PART ONE

ĀNANDA LAHARĪ

Wave of Bliss

1.

शिवः शक्त्या युक्तो यदि भवति शक्तः प्रभवितुं
न चेदेवं देवो न खलु कुशलः स्पन्दितुमपि ।

अतस्त्वामाराध्यां हरिहरविरिञ्चादिभिरपि
प्रणन्तुं स्तोतुं वा कथमकृतपुण्यः प्रभवति ॥

śivaḥ śaktyā yukto yadi bhavati śaktaḥ prabhavitum
na cedevaṃ devo na khalu kuśalaḥ spanditumapi

atastvāmārādhyāṃ hariharaviriñcādibhirapi
praṇantuṃ stotuṃ vā kathamakṛtapuṇyaḥ prabhavati

1.

Only when with her can he stir
Śakti, she's Śiva's power

Even Śiva who's a god

only prevails
when paired with her

Then how can I
Mere I

Never did a good deed
Meritless I, how

dare I even
bow to you

even praise you

You whom even the gods
Śiva Viṣṇu Brahmā

adore

2.

तनीयांसं पांसुं तव चरणपङ्केरुहभवं
विरिञ्चिः संञ्चिन्वन् विरचयति लोकानविकलम् ।

वहत्येनं शौरिः कथमपि सहस्रेण शिरसां
हरः संक्षुद्यैनं भजति भसितोद्धूलनविधिम् ॥

tanīyāṃsaṃ pāṃsuṃ tava caraṇapaṅkeruhabhavaṃ
viriñciḥ saṃcinvan viracayati lokānavikalam

vahatyenaṃ śauriḥ kathamapi sahasreṇa śirasāṃ
haraḥ saṃkṣudyainaṃ bhajati bhasitoddhūlanavidhim

2.*

Even a fleck
Even a fleck of a speck of

dust from your feet

pollen dust from
your lotus feet

Brahmā gathers it
creates worlds with it

In spite of a thousand heads
Viṣṇu barely bears it

Śiva crushes it, sprinkles it

all over
like a holy-ash ritual

3.

अविद्यानामन्तस्तिमिरमिहिरद्वीपनगरी
जडानां चैतन्यस्तबकमकरन्दस्रुतिझरी ।

दरिद्राणां चिन्तामणिगुणनिका जन्मजलधौ
निमग्नानां दंष्ट्रा मुररिपु वराहस्य भवति ॥

avidyānāmantastimiramihiradvīpanagarī
jaḍānāṃ caitanyastabakamakarandasrutijharī

daridrāṇāṃ cintāmaṇiguṇanikā janmajaladhau
nimagnānāṃ daṃṣṭrā muraripuvarāhasya bhavati

3.*

(That speck of dust
from your feet—)

Like an island town's
sun upon

the darkness within
the ignorant

A flowing stream of
honey from bouquets

waking the consciousness
of the dull lifeless

Like a string of precious
wishing gems

for the poor

For those immersed
in the ocean of rebirth

like the tusk of Varāha,
demon Mura's foe

4.

त्वदन्यः पाणिभ्यामभयवरदो दैवतगणः
त्वमेका नैवासि प्रकटितवराभीत्यभिनया ।

भयात् त्रातुं दातुं फलमपि च वाञ्छासमधिकं
शरण्ये लोकानां तव हि चरणावेव निपुणौ ॥

tvadanyaḥ pāṇibhyāmabhayavarado daivatagaṇaḥ
tvamekā naivāsi prakaṭitavarābhītyabhinayā

bhayāt trātuṃ dātuṃ phalamapi ca vāñchāsamadhikaṃ
śaraṇye lokānāṃ tava hi caraṇāveva nipuṇau

4.*

Except you

the droves of gods do mudrās
(mystic hand-signals)

abhaya mudrā to make fearless
varada mudrā to give boons

Not you

none of these
dramatics

you are the refuge
of all the worlds

To free from fear
To give more than desired

your two feet suffice

5.

हरिस्त्वामाराध्य प्रणतजनसौभाग्यजननीं
पुरा नारी भूत्वा पुररिपुमपि क्षोभमनयत् ।

स्मरोऽपि त्वां नत्वा रतिनयनलेह्येन वपुषा
मुनीनामप्यन्तः प्रभवति हि मोहाय महताम् ॥

haristvāmārādhya praṇatajanasaubhāgyajananīṃ
purā nārī bhūtvā puraripumapi kṣobhamanayat

smaro'pi tvāṃ natvā ratinayanalehyena vapuṣā
munīnāmapyantaḥ prabhavati hi mohāya mahatām

5.*

Long, long ago
only by worshipping you

Viṣṇu became a woman
called Mohinī

roused even Śiva,
foe of the cities

Kāma stirs

even the minds
of mighty sages

only by bowing
to you bodily

A body that
Rati's eyes lick

(Thanks to you, he's
visible to her)

You make good things happen
to those who bow to you

6.

धनुः पौष्पं मौर्वी मधुकरमयी पञ्च विशिखाः
वसन्तः सामन्तो मलयमरुदायोधनरथः ।

तथाप्येकः सर्वं हिमगिरिसुते कामपि कृपाम्
अपाङ्गात्ते लब्ध्वा जगदिदमनङ्गो विजयते ॥

dhanuḥ pauṣpaṃ maurvī madhukaramayī pañca viśikhāḥ
vasantaḥ sāmanto malayamarudāyodhanarathaḥ

tathāpyekaḥ sarvaṃ himagirisute kāmapi kṛpām
apāṅgātte labdhvā jagadidamanaṅgo vijayate

6.*

Although Kāma
has only

a bow with a
bowstring of bees

for arrows, five flowers

for a war-chariot, the (mild)
south wind

as charioteer,
the spring season (a novice)

O daughter of
the snow mountain

One sidelong glance
from you and

bodiless Kāma wins over
this entire world

7.

क्वणत्काञ्चीदामा करिकलभकुम्भस्तननता
परिक्षीणा मध्ये परिणतशरच्चन्द्रवदना ।

धनुर्बाणान् पाशं सृणिमपि दधाना करतलैः
पुरस्तादास्तां नः पुरमथितुराहोपुरुषिका ॥

kvaṇatkāñcīdāmā karikalabhakumbhastananatā
parikṣīṇā madhye pariṇataśaraccandravadanā

dhanurbāṇān pāśaṃ sṛṇimapi dadhānā karatalaiḥ
purastādāstāṃ naḥ puramathiturāhopuruṣikā

7.*

Jingle girdle askew
Slim waist sashay

She stoops, for
bosom's heavy

like the swollen lobes
of an elephant's forehead

Face like the radiant
autumn full moon

holding a bow, noose, goad
and arrows in her hands

Oh the pride of
Śiva, crusher of cities

may she be
before us

8.

सुधासिन्धोर्मध्ये सुरविटपिवाटीपरिवृते
मणिद्वीपे नीपोपवनवति चिन्तामणिगृहे ।

शिवाकारे मञ्चे परमशिवपर्यङ्कनिलयां
भजन्ति त्वां धन्याः कतिचन चिदानन्दलहरीम् ॥

sudhāsindhormadhye suraviṭapivāṭīparivṛte
maṇidvīpe nīpopavanavati cintāmaṇigṛhe

śivākāre mañce paramaśivaparyaṅkanilayāṃ
bhajanti tvāṃ dhanyāḥ katicana cidānandalaharīm

8.

In the middle of an ocean
of ambrosial joy

Maṇidvīpa, an island
of precious gems

enclosed by groves
of wish-fulfilling trees

In a garden of
kadamba trees

in a house made of
cintāmaṇi gems

resting upon a couch
of prone Śiva

on pedestals of Brahmā
Viṣṇu, Rudra and Īśvara

you

A blissful wave
of consciousness

only the fortunate
worship

9.

महीं मूलाधारे कमपि मणिपूरे हुतवहं
स्थितं स्वाधिष्ठाने हृदि मरुतमाकाशमुपरि ।

मनोऽपि भ्रूमध्ये सकलमपि भित्त्वा कुलपथं
सहस्रारे पद्मे सह रहसि पत्या विहरसे ॥

mahīṃ mūlādhāre kamapi maṇipūre hutavahaṃ
sthitaṃ svādhiṣṭhāne hṛdi marutamākāśamupari

mano'pi bhrūmadhye sakalamapi bhittvā kulapathaṃ
sahasrāre padme saha rahasi patyā viharase

9.*

You rise along the spirit's
arterial passage in the spine
suṣumnā nāḍī

You pierce all energy centres

earth in mūlādhāra
water in maṇipūra
fire in svādhiṣṭhāna
air in heart anāhata
ether above that in viśuddha
mind between brows ājñā

In the lotus of one thousand petals
sahasrāra the crown

you dance with your husband
in secret

10.

सुधाधारासारैश्चरणयुगलान्तर्विगलितैः
प्रपञ्चं सिञ्चन्ती पुनरपि रसाम्नायमहसः ।

अवाप्य स्वां भूमिं भुजगनिभमध्युष्टवलयं
स्वमात्मानं कृत्वा स्वपिषि कुलकुण्डे कुहरिणि ॥

sudhādhārāsāraiścaraṇayugalāntarvigalitaiḥ
prapañcaṃ siñcantī punarapi rasāmnāyamahasaḥ

avāpya svāṃ bhūmiṃ bhujaganibhamadhyuṣṭavalayaṃ
svamātmānaṃ kṛtvā svapiṣi kulakuṇḍe kuhariṇi

10.

Streams of nectar essence
from between your soles

sprinkle the world
(of nerves in the body)

And again from great lunar
heights (the crown)

returning to your own ground
you make yourself coil

three and a half times
like a serpent, sleep
in the pit

at the root cakra
mūlādhāra

11.

चतुर्भिः श्रीकण्ठैः शिवयुवतिभिः पञ्चभिरपि
प्रभिन्नाभिः शम्भोर्नवभिरपि मूलप्रकृतिभिः ।

चतुश्चत्वारिंशद्वसुदलकलाश्रत्रिवलय-
त्रिरेखाभिः सार्धं तव शरणकोणाः परिणताः ॥

caturbhiḥ śrīkaṇṭhaiḥ śivayuvatibhiḥ pañcabhirapi
prabhinnābhiḥ śambhornavabhirapi mūlaprakṛtibhiḥ

catuścatvāriṃśadvasudalakalāśratrivalaya-
trirekhābhiḥ sārdhaṃ tava śaraṇakoṇāḥ pariṇatāḥ

11.*

Pierced
by the centre bindu

four Śiva and
five Śakti make nine
triangles

distinct, basic elements

and with petals eight
and sixteen

in three and three circles
and lines

four and forty angles
complete your abode

12.

त्वदीयं सौन्दर्यं तुहिनगिरिकन्ये तुलयितुं
कवीन्द्राः कल्पन्ते कथमपि विरिञ्चिप्रभृतयः ।

यदालोकौत्सुक्यादमरललना यान्ति मनसा
तपोभिर्दुष्प्रापामपि गिरिशसायुज्यपदवीम् ॥

tvadīyaṃ saundaryaṃ tuhinagirikanye tulayituṃ
kavīndrāḥ kalpante kathamapi viriñciprabhṛtayaḥ

yadālokautsukyādamaralalanā yānti manasā
tapobhirduṣprāpāmapi giriśasāyujyapadavīm

12.

O daughter of
the snow mountain

Even the best of poets
Brahmā and others

can barely imagine how
to appreciate your beauty

Eager to gaze at it

celestial nymphs
become one with Śiva
imaginatively

Śiva, unattainable
even with austerities

13.

नरं वर्षीयांसं नयनविरसं नर्मसु जडं
तवापाङ्गालोके पतितमनुधावन्ति शतशः ।

गलद्वेणीबन्धाः कुचकलशविस्रस्तसिचया
हठात् त्रुट्यत्काञ्च्यो विगलितदुकूला युवतयः ॥

naraṃ varṣīyāṃsaṃ nayanavirasaṃ narmasu jaḍaṃ
tavāpāṅgāloke patitamanudhāvanti śataśaḥ

galadveṇībandhāḥ kucakalaśavisrastasicayā
haṭhāt truṭyatkāñcyo vigalitadukūlā yuvatayaḥ

13.

Śiva's old, ugly
impotent

The moment
your sidelong glance
falls on him

hundreds of young women
run after him

Hair-knots undone

blouses loosening on pitcher-like bosoms
skirts slipping from snapped girdles

hundreds of young women
run after him

14.

क्षितौ षट्पञ्चाशद् द्विसमधिकपञ्चाशदुदके
हुताशे द्वाषष्टिश्चतुरधिकपञ्चाशदनिले ।

दिवि द्विःषट्त्रिंशन्मनसि च चतुःषष्टिरिति ये
मयूखास्तेषामप्युपरि तव पादाम्बुजयुगम् ॥

kṣitau ṣaṭpañcāśad dvisamadhikapañcāśadudake
hutāśe dvāṣaṣṭiścaturadhikapañcāśadanile

divi dviḥṣaṭtriṃśanmanasi ca catuḥṣaṣṭiriti ye
mayūkhāsteṣāmapyupari tava pādāmbujayugam

14.*

Your rays:

Fifty-six in earth
mūlādhāra cakra

Fifty-two in water
maṇipūra cakra

Sixty-two in fire
svādhiṣṭhāna cakra

Fifty-four in air
anāhata cakra

Seventy-two in ether
viśuddha cakra

Sixty-four in the mind
ājñā cakra

And above them all
(altogether rays 360)

your lotus feet
sahasrāra cakra

15.

शरज्ज्योत्स्नाशुद्धां शशियुतजटाजूटमकुटां
वरत्रासत्राणस्फटिकघटिकापुस्तककराम् ।

सकृन्न त्वा नत्वा कथमिव सतां संनिदधते
मधुक्षीरद्राक्षामधुरिमधुरीणाः फणितयः ॥

śarajjyotsnāśuddhāṃ śaśiyutajaṭājūṭamakuṭāṃ
varatrāsatrāṇasphaṭikaghaṭikāpustakakarām

sakṛnna tvā natvā kathamiva satāṃ saṃnidadhate
madhukṣīradrākṣāmadhurimadhurīṇāḥ phaṇitayaḥ

15.*

You're bright as
the autumn moon

The moon crowns
your tresses

A book in one hand
Crystal rosary in another

A hand granting wishes
Another, fearlessness

Truth-seekers who bow
to you just once

cannot but be endowed
with a tongue, sweet

as honey, milk
and grapes

16.

कवीन्द्राणां चेतःकमलवनबालातपरुचिं
भजन्ते ये सन्तः कतिचिदरुणामेव भवतीम् ।

विरिञ्चिप्रेयस्यास्तरुणतरश्रृङ्गारलहरी-
गभीराभिर्वाग्भिर्विदधति सतां रञ्जनममी ॥

kavīndrāṇāṃ cetaḥkamalavanabālātaparuciṃ
bhajante ye santaḥ katicidaruṇāmeva bhavatīm

viriñcipreyasyāstaruṇataraśṛṅgāralaharī-
gabhīrābhirvāgbhirvidadhati satāṃ rañjanamamī

16.*

Your reddish form

surges like a fresh wave
of passion (śṛṅgāra)

from Brahmā's beloved
Sarasvatī

The wise few who
worship you thus

please truth-seekers
with profound words

The minds of
great poets blossom

like lotus fields
in the morning sun

17.

सवित्रीभिर्वाचां शशिमणिशिलाभङ्गरुचिभिः
वशिन्याद्याभिस्त्वां सह जननि सञ्चिन्तयति यः ।

स कर्ता काव्यानां भवति महतां भङ्गिरुचिभिः
वचोभिर्वाग्देवीवदनकमलामोदमधुरैः ॥

savitrībhirvācāṃ śaśimaṇiśilābhaṅgarucibhir-
vaśinyādyābhistvāṃ saha janani sañcintayati yaḥ

sa kartā kāvyānāṃ bhavati mahatāṃ bhaṅgirucibhir-
vacobhirvāgdevīvadanakamalāmodamadhuraiḥ

17.[*]

Mother,

he who meditates
on you

with Vaśinī and cohort
(deities of speech)

who gleam like
moonstone flakes

he becomes the composer
of great, well-crafted poems

poems with the honeyed fragrance
of the lotus-like mouth

of the goddess of speech,
Sarasvatī

18.

तनुच्छायाभिस्ते तरुणतरणिश्रीसरणिभिः
दिवं सर्वामुर्वीमरुणिमनि मग्नां स्मरति यः ।

भवन्त्यस्य त्रस्यद्वनहरिणशालीननयनाः
सहोर्वश्या वश्याः कति कति न गीर्वाणगणिकाः ॥

tanucchāyābhiste taruṇataraṇiśrīsaraṇibhir-
divaṃ sarvāmurvīmaruṇimani magnāṃ smarati yaḥ

bhavantyasya trasyadvanahariṇaśālīnanayanāḥ
sahorvaśyā vaśyāḥ kati kati na gīrvāṇagaṇikāḥ

18.*

Your body's hue:

Glorious rays, pathways
of the rising sun

sky and all earth
steeped deep red

Among celestial
courtesans

with shy eyes like
timid does in the wild

No one, not even
Urvaśī is not

captivated by
he who meditates

on your body's hue

19.

मुखं बिन्दुं कृत्वा कुचयुगमधस्तस्य तदधो
हरार्धं ध्यायेद्यो हरमहिषि ते मन्मथकलाम् ।

ससद्यः संक्षोभं नयति वनिता इत्यतिलघु
त्रिलोकीमप्याशु भ्रमयति रवीन्दुस्तनयुगाम् ॥

mukhaṃ binduṃ kṛtvā kucayugamadhastasya tadadho
harārdhaṃ dhyāyedyo haramahiṣi te manmathakalām

sa sadyaḥ saṃkṣobhaṃ nayati vanitā ityatilaghu
trilokīmapyāśu bhramayati ravīndustanayugām

19.*

O Śiva's queen

He who meditates on
your subtle form

Your face as bindu (the
centre dot in Śrīyantra)

Your breasts below that
(forming a triangle)

Below that, Śiva's
other half

(the inverted triangle
of yoni)

He who thinks of
your subtle form

stirs any woman at once
—easy—and instantly

makes Trilokī dizzy,
the cosmic woman

whose breasts are
the sun and moon

20.

किरन्तीमङ्गेभ्यः किरणनिकुरम्बामृतरसं
हृदि त्वामाधत्ते हिमकरशिलामूर्तिमिव यः ।

स सर्पाणां दर्पं शमयति शकुन्ताधिप इव
ज्वरप्लुष्टान् दृष्ट्या सुखयति सुधाधारसिरया ॥

kirantīmaṅgebhyaḥ kiraṇanikurumbāmṛtarasaṃ
hṛdi tvāmādhatte himakaraśilāmūrtimiva yaḥ

sa sarpāṇāṃ darpaṃ śamayati śakuntādhipa iva
jvarapluṣṭān dṛṣṭyā sukhayati sudhādhārasirayā

20.*

He who holds you
in his heart

in the image of
cool moonstone

your limbs exuding
a mass of light

ambrosia

He subdues the gall
of serpents

like Garuḍa
king of raptors

Cures a raging fever
with a glance

with the nerve
that rains nectar

21.

तटिल्लेखातन्वीं तपनशशिवैश्वानरमयीं
निषण्णां षण्णामप्युपरि कमलानां तव कलाम् ।

महापद्माटव्यां मृदितमलमायेन मनसा
महान्तः पश्यन्तो दधति परमाह्लादलहरीम् ॥

taṭillekhātanvīṃ tapanaśaśivaiśvānaramayīṃ
niṣaṇṇāṃ ṣaṇṇāmapyupari kamalānāṃ tava kalām

mahāpadmāṭavyāṃ mṛditamalamāyena manasā
mahāntaḥ paśyanto dadhati paramāhlādalaharīm

21.*

A lightning streak
of sun, moon and fire

your energy

seated in the great lotus forest
of thousand petals
(sahasrāra cakra)

high above even the six
lotuses (cakras)

Seeing
your energy

great yogis whose
minds are free

of impurities
illusions

experience a tide
of supreme bliss

22.

भवानि त्वं दासे मयि वितर दृष्टिं सकरुणा-
-मिति स्तोतुं वाञ्छन् कथयति भवानि त्वमिति यः ।

तदैव त्वं तस्मै दिशसि निजसायुज्यपदवीं
मुकुन्दब्रह्मेन्द्रस्फुटमकुटनीराजितपदाम् ॥

bhavāni tvaṃ dāse mayi vitara dṛṣṭiṃ sakaruṇā-
-miti stotuṃ vāñchan kathayati bhavāni tvamiti yaḥ

tadaiva tvaṃ tasmai diśasi nijasāyujyapadavīṃ
mukundabrahmendrasphuṭamakuṭanīrājitapadām

22.*

Even before he
who wants to praise says:

'O Bhavānī extend

a compassionate look
at your servant'

you hear the first part:

'Bhavāni tvaṃ…'
'May I be you…'

At once you grant

the state of oneness
at your shining feet

Shining as if the crowns of
Viṣṇu, Brahmā and Indra

are lamps offered
in worship

23.

त्वया हृत्वा वामं वपुरपरितृप्तेन मनसा
शरीरार्धं शम्भोरपरमपि शङ्के हृतमभूत् ।

यदेतत्त्वद्रूपं सकलमरुणाभं त्रिनयनं
कुचाभ्यामानम्रं कुटिलशशिचूडालमकुटम् ॥

tvayā hṛtvā vāmaṃ vapuraparitṛptena manasā
śarīrārdhaṃ śambhoraparamapi śaṅke hṛtamabhūt

yadetattvadrūpaṃ sakalamaruṇābhaṃ trinayanaṃ
kucābhyāmānamraṃ kuṭilaśaśicūḍālamakuṭam

23.[*]

I wonder if

after usurping the left half
of Śiva's body

discontented

you took
the other half

It explains this look:

crimson glow all over
stooping due to breasts

(and yet like Śiva)
three-eyed, crown awry

moon crested in your hair

24.

जगत्सूते धाता हरिरवति रुद्रः क्षपयते
तिरस्कुर्वन्नेतत्स्वमपि वपुरीशस्तिरयति ।

सदापूर्वः सर्वं तदिदमनुगृह्णाति च शिव-
स्तवाज्ञामालम्ब्य क्षणचलितयोर्भ्रूलतिकयोः ॥

jagatsūte dhātā hariravati rudraḥ kṣapayate
tiraskurvannetatsvamapi vapurīśastirayati

sadāpūrvaḥ sarvaṃ tadidamanugṛhṇāti ca śiva-
stavājñāmālambya kṣaṇacalitayorbhrūlatikayoḥ

24.*

The universe:

Brahmā creates
Hari preserves
Rudra destroys

Īśa dissolves all of them
and his own body

Then primeval Sadāśiva
restores it all
on cue—

the quick flick of
your eyebrow-tendrils

25.

त्रयाणां देवानां त्रिगुणजनितानां तव शिवे
भवेत् पूजा पूजा तव चरणयोर्या विरचिता ।

तथा हि त्वत्पादोद्वहनमणिपीठस्य निकटे
स्थिता ह्येते शश्वन्मुकुलितकरोत्तंसमकुटाः ॥

trayāṇāṃ devānāṃ triguṇajanitānāṃ tava śive
bhavet pūjā pūjā tava caraṇayoryā viracitā

tathā hi tvatpādodvahanamaṇipīṭhasya nikaṭe
sthitā hyete śaśvanmukulitakarottaṃsamakuṭāḥ

25.*

O auspicious one

Puja performed
to your feet

as good as puja
of Brahmā, Viṣṇu, Śiva

the three gods created
by your three aspects

No wonder they stand
in wait forever, near

the gem-studded stool
that supports your feet

hands folded like buds
above their diadems

26.

विरिञ्चिः पञ्चत्वं व्रजति हरिराप्नोति विरतिं
विनाशं कीनाशो भजति धनदो याति निधनम् ।

वितन्द्री माहेन्द्री विततिरपि सम्मीलितदृशा
महासंहारेऽस्मिन् विहरति सति त्वत्पतिरसौ ॥

viriñciḥ pañcatvaṃ vrajati harirāpnoti viratiṃ
vināśaṃ kīnāśo bhajati dhanado yāti nidhanam

vitandrī māhendrī vitatirapi sammīlitadṛśā
mahāsaṃhāre'smin viharati sati tvatpatirasau

26.*

Brahmā returns to the five elements
Viṣṇu comes to a pause

Yama has his share of death
Kubera's finished

Indra's eyes though numerous
fall shut, weary

In this great dissolution
O chaste one, only

your husband, he
plays

27.

जपो जल्पः शिल्पं सकलमपि मुद्राविरचना
गतिः प्रादक्षिण्यक्रमणमशनाद्याहुतिविधिः ।

प्रणामस्संवेशस्सुखमखिलमात्मार्पणदृशा
सपर्यापर्यायस्तव भवतु यन्मे विलसितम् ॥

japo jalpaḥ śilpaṃ sakalamapi mudrāviracanā
gatiḥ prādakṣiṇyakramaṇamaśanādyāhutividhiḥ

praṇāmah saṃveśaḥ sukhamakhilamātmārpaṇadṛśā
saparyāparyāyastava bhavatu yanme vilasitam

27.

Let my chatter be
the repetition of your name
mantra japa

Let my activity enact
mystic signs
mudrā

Let walking be the steps
of circumambulation
pradakṣiṇa

Let all food be
offerings to sacred fire
āhuti

May laying down be
a prostration to you
praṇāma

Let all pleasures that
give me comfort be

like an offering of
my own self
ātmārpaṇa

May whatever I enjoy be yours
like recurring prayers

(My favourite verse.)

28.

सुधामप्यास्वाद्य प्रतिभयजरामृत्युहरिणीं
विपद्यन्ते विश्वे विधिशतमखाद्या दिविषदः ।

करालं यत्क्ष्वेलं कबलितवतः कालकलना
न शम्भोस्तन्मूलं तव जननि ताटङ्कमहिमा ॥

sudhāmapyāsvādya pratibhayajarāmṛtyuhariṇīṃ
vipadyante viśve vidhiśatamakhādyā diviṣadaḥ

karālaṃ yatkṣvelaṃ kabalitavataḥ kālakalanā
na śambhostanmūlaṃ tava janani tāṭaṅkamahimā

28.*

O Mother

In spite of tasting nectar
that destroys

dreadful decrepitude
and death

Brahmā, Indra and other
gods who live

in heaven
do die

But in spite of eating
vile poison

Śiva is unravaged
by time

It's the magic power
of your earrings

29.

किरीटं वैरिञ्चं परिहर पुरः कैटभभिदः
कठोरे कोटीरे स्खलसि जहि जम्भारिमकुटम् ।

प्रणम्रेष्वेतेषु प्रसभमुपयातस्य भवनं
भवस्याभ्युत्थाने तव परिजनोक्तिर्विजयते ॥

kirīṭaṃ vairiñcaṃ parihara puraḥ kaiṭabhabhidaḥ
kaṭhore koṭīre skhalasi jahi jambhārimakuṭam

praṇamreṣveteṣu prasabhamupayātasya bhavanaṃ
bhavasyābhyutthāne tava parijanoktirvijayate

29.*

Upon Śiva's arrival

at your mansion where
the gods prostrate

as you jump up at once
(to receive him)

your attendants' voices
crow:

'That's Brahmā's crown
ahead, keep off'

'You'll trip on the hard crown
of Kaitabha-killer Viṣṇu'

'Avoid the crown of
Jambha's enemy Indra!'

30.

स्वदेहोद्भूताभिर्घृणिभिरणिमाद्याभिरभितो
निषेव्ये नित्ये त्वामहमिति सदा भावयति यः ।

किमाश्चर्यं तस्य त्रिनयनसमृद्धिं तृणयतो
महासंवर्ताग्निर्विरचयति निराजनविधिम् ॥

svadehodbhūtābhirghṛṇibhiraṇimādyābhirabhito
niṣevye nitye tvāmahamiti sadā bhāvayati yaḥ

kimāścaryaṃ tasya trinayanasamṛddhiṃ tṛṇayato
mahāsaṃvartāgnirviracayati nīrājanavidhim

30.

O eternal, revered one

You're flanked by
rays

emanating
from your own body

powers like aṇimā
who bestows

the power to become
miniscule

For him who always feels
'I am you'

Śiva's glory is trivial
like a blade of grass

It's no surprise
the fire of annihilation

performs an offering
of light to him

31.

चतुष्षष्ट्या तन्त्रैः सकलमतिसन्धाय भुवनं
स्थितस्तत्तत्सिद्धिप्रसवपरतन्त्रैः पशुपतिः ।

पुनस्त्वन्निर्बन्धादखिलपुरुषार्थैकघटना-
स्वतन्त्रं ते तन्त्रं क्षितितलमवातीतरदिदम् ॥

catuḥṣaṣṭyā tantraiḥ sakalamatisandhāya bhuvanaṃ
sthitastattatsiddhiprasavaparatantraiḥ paśupatiḥ

punastvannirbandhādakhilapuruṣārthaikaghaṭanā-
svatantraṃ te tantraṃ kṣititalamavātītaradidam

31.*

Śiva duped
the entire world

with sixty-four tantras

each has only
a mundane power

When you insisted

he revealed this
on the face of the earth

this, your tantra, Śrīvidyā
independent of other tantras

All human goals
accomplished in one go

32.

शिवः शक्तिः कामः क्षितिरथ रविः शीतकिरणः
स्मरो हंसः शक्रस्तदनु च परामारहरयः ।

अमी हृल्लेखाभिस्तिसृभिरवसानेषु घटिता
भजन्ते वर्णास्ते तव जननि नामावयवताम् ॥

śivaḥ śaktiḥ kāmaḥ kṣitiratha raviḥ śītakiraṇaḥ
smaro haṃsaḥ śakrastadanu ca parāmāraharayaḥ

amī hṛllekhābhistisṛbhiravasāneṣu ghaṭitā
bhajante varṇāste tava janani nāmāvayavatām

32.*

Mother,

linked by three hrīṁs

these decoded syllables
formulate the parts
of your name

Ka E Ī La Hrīṃ Ha Sa Ka Ha La Hrīṃ Sa Ka La Hrīṃ

Ka from Śiva
E from Śakti
Ī from Love
La from Earth
Hrīṁ

and

Ha from Sun
Sa from Moon
Ka from Love
Ha from Swan, a realized being
La from Indra, chief of the Gods
Hrīṁ

and again

Sa from Brahmā
Ka from Love
La from Viṣṇu
Hrīṁ

33.

स्मरं योनिं लक्ष्मीं त्रितयमिदमादौ तव मनो-
र्निधायैके नित्ये निरवधिमहाभोगरसिकाः ।

भजन्ति त्वां चिन्तामणिगुननिबद्धाक्षवलयाः
शिवाग्नौ जुह्वन्तः सुरभिघृतधाराहुतिशतैः ॥

smaraṃ yoniṃ lakṣmīṃ tritayamidamādau tava manor-
nidhāyaike nitye niravadhimahābhogarasikāḥ

bhajanti tvāṃ cintāmaṇiguṇanibaddhākṣavalayāḥ
śivāgnau juhvantaḥ surabhighṛtadhārāhutiśataiḥ

33.*

O eternal one,

some who desire
abundant non-stop bliss

place klīṁ hrīṁ śrīṁ
before your mantra

adore you with rosaries
alphabet rosaries

holding the power
of wishing gems

do hundreds of oblations
internally

in the fire of the heart
with streams of ghee

made from the milk
of the wish-fulfilling cow

34.

शरीरं त्वं शम्भोः शशिमिहिरवक्षोरुहयुगं
तवात्मानं मन्ये भगवति नवात्मानमनघम् ।

अतश्शेषश्शेषीत्ययमुभयसाधारणतया
स्थितः सम्बन्धो वां समरसपरानन्दपरयोः ॥

śarīraṃ tvaṃ śambhoḥ śaśimihiravakṣoruhayugaṃ
tavātmānaṃ manye bhagavati navātmānamanagham

ataḥ śeṣaḥ śeṣītyayamubhayasādhāraṇatayā
sthitaḥ sambandho vāṃ samarasaparānandaparayoḥ

34.*

O Goddess,

the sun and moon
your breasts

You are Śiva's body
I believe

your very self
is Śiva

of nine attributes
flawless

As for who's primary
who secondary

your relationship stands
equal

by what you share:
transcendence, and bliss

35.

मनस्त्वं व्योम त्वं मरुदसि मरुत्सारथिरसि
त्वमापस्त्वं भूमिस्त्वयि परिणतायां न हि परम् ।

त्वमेव स्वात्मानं परिणमयितुं विश्ववपुषा
चिदानन्दाकारं शिवयुवति भावेन बिभृषे ॥

manastvaṃ vyoma tvaṃ marudasi marutsārathirasi
tvamāpastvaṃ bhūmistvayi pariṇatāyāṃ na hi param

tvameva svātmānaṃ pariṇamayituṃ viśvavapuṣā
cidānandākāraṃ śivayuvati bhāvena bibhṛṣe

35.

You are mind

You are space

You are wind

You are fire whose
charioteer is wind

You are water

You are earth

There is nothing beyond
your full manifestation

You, yourself,

expression of
blissful consciousness

you assume the role
of Śiva's damsel

to become fully manifest
through the physical

universe

36.

तवाज्ञाचक्रस्थं तपनशशिकोटिद्युतिधरं
परं शम्भुं वन्दे परिमिलितपार्श्वं परचिता ।

यमाराध्यन् भक्त्या रविशशिशुचीनामविषये
निरालोकेऽलोके निवसति हि भालोकभुवने ॥

tavājñācakrastham tapanaśaśikoṭidyutidharaṃ
paraṃ śambhuṃ vande parimilitapārśvaṃ paracitā

yamārādhyan bhaktyā raviśaśiśucīnāmaviṣaye
nirāloke'loke nivasati hi bhālokabhuvane

36.[*]

I bow to the supreme
lord Śambhu

anchored in your ājñā cakra
between your brows

carrying the light of
crores of suns and moons

surrounded by supreme
consciousness (paracitā)

Adoring him with devotion
one remains

in a self-luminous state
beyond sun moon fire

in a place that
cannot be perceived

37.

विशुद्धौ ते शुद्धस्फटिकविशदं व्योमजनकं
शिवं सेवे देवीमपि शिवसमानव्यवसिताम् ।

ययोः कान्त्या यान्त्याः शशिकिरणसारूप्यसरणे-
विधूतान्तर्ध्वान्ता विलसति चकोरीव जगती ॥

viśuddhau te śuddhasphaṭikaviśadaṃ vyomajanakaṃ
śivaṃ seve devīmapi śivasamānavyavasitām

yayoḥ kāntyā yāntyāḥ śaśikiraṇasārūpyasaraṇe-
vidhūtāntardhvāntā vilasati cakorīva jagatī

37.

In the viśuddha cakra
at your throat

I bow to Śiva and Śakti

Śiva, flawless as pure crystal,
source of ether

Śakti, equally active

Cleared of inner darkness

the world
like a cakora bird

thrives in their
radiance

emanating like
flowing moon rays

38.

समुन्मीलत् संवित् कमलमकरन्दैकरसिकं
भजे हंसद्वन्द्वं किमपि महतां मानसचरम् ।

यदालापादष्टादशगुणितविद्यापरिणति-
र्यदादत्ते दोषाद् गुणमखिलमद्भ्यः पय इव ॥

samunmīlat saṃvit kamalamakarandaikarasikaṃ
bhaje haṃsadvandvaṃ kimapi mahatāṃ mānasacaram

yadālāpādaṣṭādaśaguṇitavidyāpariṇatir-
yadādatte doṣādguṇamakhilamadbhyaḥ paya iva

38.*

I adore the swan pair

who glide in the hearts
of great people

who only relish
the knowledge-nectar

of an open
lotus heart

from whose calls evolve
eighteen sciences

who reclaim all good qualities
from defects

like milk from water

39.

तव स्वाधिष्ठाने हुतवहमधिष्ठाय निरतं
तमीडे संवर्तं जननि महतीं तां च समयाम् ।

यदालोके लोकान् दहति महति क्रोधकलिते
दयार्द्रा या दृष्टिः शिशिरमुपचारं रचयति ॥

tava svādhiṣṭhāne hutavahamadhiṣṭhāya niratam
tamīḍe saṃvartaṃ janani mahatīṃ tāṃ ca samayām

yadāloke lokān dahati mahati krodhakalite
dayārdrā yā dṛṣṭiḥ śiśiramupacāraṃ racayati

39.*

Invoking the fire of annihilation
in your svādhiṣṭhāna cakra

I praise him, Saṃvarta,
intensely

And I praise you, O
great mother, Samayā

whose glance moist with compassion
creates a cool remedy

when his look full of intense anger
burns worlds

40.

तटित्त्वन्तं शक्त्या तिमिरपरिपन्थिफुरणया
स्फुरन्नानारत्नाभरणपरिणद्धेन्द्रधनुषम् ।

तव श्यामं मेघं कमपि मणिपूरैकशरणं
निषेवे वर्षन्तं हरमिहिरतप्तं त्रिभुवनम् ॥

taṭittvantaṃ śaktyā timiraparipanthisphuraṇayā
sphurannānāratnābharaṇapariṇaddhendradhanuṣam

tava śyāmaṃ meghaṃ kamapi maṇipūraikaśaraṇaṃ
niṣeve varṣantaṃ haramihirataptaṃ tribhuvanam

40.*

I worship the indescribable
blue cloud

that rains over three worlds
sun-scorched by Hara

that resides only in your
navel (maṇipūra cakra)

its darkness illuminated
by lightning (Śakti)

flashing a rainbow of all sorts
of gems and ornaments

41.

तवाधारे मूले सह समयया लास्यपरया
नवात्मानं मन्ये नवरसमहाताण्डवनटम् ।

उभाभ्यामेताभ्यामुदयविधिमुद्दिश्य दयया
सनाथाभ्यां जज्ञे जनकजननीमज्जगदिदम् ॥

tavādhāre mūle saha samayayā lāsyaparayā
navātmānaṃ manye navarasa mahātāṇḍavanaṭam

ubhābhyāmetābhyāmudayavidhimuddiśya dayayā
sanāthābhyāṃ jajñe janakajananīmajjagadidam

41.*

In your root cakra (mūlādhāra)
I meditate

on nine-faceted Śiva who dances
the grand masculine dance (tāṇḍava)

of nine aesthetic emotions (rasas)
with Śakti who dances

the feminine dance
overcome with feeling

From these two

in a compassionate union
for the sake of creation

the world
fathered and mothered

is born

PART TWO

SAUNDARYA LAHARĪ

Wave of Beauty

42.

गतैर्माणिक्यत्वं गगनमणिभिः सान्द्रघटितं
किरीटं ते हैमं हिमगिरिसुते कीर्तयति यः ।

स नीडेयच्छायाच्छुरणशबलं चन्द्रशकलं
धनुः शौनासीरं किमिति न निबध्नाति धिषणाम् ॥

gatairmāṇikyatvaṃ gaganamaṇibhiḥ sāndraghaṭitaṃ
kirīṭaṃ te haimaṃ himagirisute kīrtayati yaḥ

sa nīḍeyacchāyācchuraṇaśabalaṃ candraśakalaṃ
dhanuḥ śaunāsīraṃ kimiti na nibadhnāti dhiṣaṇām

42.*

O daughter

of the lord of the snow mountain
(Himavān of the Himalayas)

Whoever sings praise
of your golden crown

densely studded with
ruby-like sky-gems
(constellations)

will his mind not surmise
its sliver-moon shape

the dappled spread
in its shade

as Indra's bow
(rainbow)?

43.

धुनोतु ध्वान्तं नस्तुलितदलितेन्दीवरवनं
घनस्निग्धश्लक्ष्णं चिकुरनिकुरुम्बं तव शिवे ।

यदीयं सौरभ्यं सहजमुपलब्धुं सुमनसो
वसन्त्यस्मिन् मन्ये वलमथनवाटीविटपिनाम् ॥

dhunotu dhvāntaṃ nastulitadalitendīvaravanaṃ
ghanasnigdhaślakṣṇaṃ cikuranikurumbaṃ tava śive

yadīyaṃ saurabhyaṃ sahajamupalabdhuṃ sumanaso
vasantyasmin manye valamathanavāṭīviṭapinām

43.*

O Śiva's consort

Your thick tresses are
dense, silken, glossy

like a forest of full-
blossomed blue lotuses

I believe

divine flowers
of plants in the garden

of Indra, the crusher of Vala,
reside here (in your hair)

to gather its innate
fragrance

May your tresses clear
our ignorance

44.

तनोतु क्षेमं नस्तव वदनसौन्दर्यलहरी-
परीवाहस्रोतःसरणिरिव सीमन्तसरणिः ।

वहन्ती सिन्दूरं प्रबलकबरीभारतिमिर-
द्विषां बृन्दैर्बन्दीकृतमिव नवीनार्ककिरणम् ॥

tanotu kṣemaṃ nastava vadanasaundaryalaharī-
parīvāhasrotaḥsaraṇiriva sīmantasaraṇiḥ

vahantī sindūraṃ prabalakabarībhāratimira-
dviṣāṃ bṛndairbandīkṛtamiva navīnārkakiraṇam

44.*

Your hair parting
a path

for the overflow of waves
of beauty from your ocean face

A path bearing red kuṅkum
like a ray of rising sun

as if held prisoner
by enemies

on either side, by heavy
dark, dense tresses

May your hair parting
show us the way

45.

अरालैः स्वाभाव्यादलिकलभसश्रीभिरलकैः
परीतं ते वक्त्रं परिहसति पङ्केरुहरुचिम् ।

दरस्मेरे यस्मिन् दशनरुचिकिञ्जल्करुचिरे
सुगन्धौ माद्यन्ति स्मरदहनचक्षुर्मधुलिहः ॥

arālaiḥ svābhāvyādalikalabhasaśrībhiralakaiḥ
parītaṃ te vaktraṃ parihasati paṅkeruharucim

darasmere yasmin daśanarucikiñjalkarucire
sugandhau mādyanti smaradahanacakṣurmadhulihaḥ

45.*

Locks naturally curly
like lovely baby bees

surrounding your face
mock the mud-born lotus

In a slight smile, teeth
neat as lotus stamens

madden with their fragrance
the honey-licker eyes

—bee eyes—of Śiva
that burned Kāma

46.

ललाटं लावण्यद्युतिविमलमाभाति तव यत-
द्वितीयं तन्मन्ये मकुटघटितं चन्द्रशकलम् ।

विपर्यास न्यासादुभयमपि सम्भूय च मिथः
सुधालेपस्यूतिः परिणमति राकाहिमकरः ॥

lalāṭaṃ lāvaṇyadyutivimalamābhāti tava yat-
dvitīyaṃ tanmanye makuṭaghaṭitaṃ candraśakalam

viparyāsa nyāsādubhayamapi sambhūya ca mithaḥ
sudhālepasyūtiḥ pariṇamati rākāhimakaraḥ

46.

Splendid, spotless, your
pretty forehead shines

I think of it as a second
crescent moon

fitted in your crown

Both crescents flipped
ends joined

combined with each other
they become

a full moon sac
ambrosia drip

47.

भ्रुवौ भुग्ने किञ्चिद्भुवनभयभङ्गव्यसनिनि
त्वदीये नेत्राभ्यां मधुकररुचिभ्यां धृतगुणम् ।

धनुर्मन्ये सव्येतरकरगृहीतं रतिपतेः
प्रकोष्ठे मुष्टौ च स्थगयति निगूढान्तरमुमे ॥

bhruvau bhugne kiñcidbhuvanabhayabhaṅgavyasanini
tvadīye netrābhyāṃ madhukararucibhyāṃ dhṛtaguṇam

dhanurmanye savyetarakaragṛhītaṃ ratipateḥ
prakoṣṭhe muṣṭau ca sthagayati nigūḍhāntaramume

47.*

O Uma, Śakti, busy
causing fear in the world

When your eyebrows
are somewhat arched

strung with your eyes
like bees

I imagine a bow gripped
in the left hand of

Kāma, consort of Rati,
his fist and forearm over

the centre of the bow
of your brows

48.

अहः सूते सव्यं तव नयनमर्कात्मकतया
त्रियामां वामं ते सृजति रजनीनायकतया ।

तृतीया ते दृष्टिर्दरदलितहेमाम्बुजरुचिः
समाधत्ते सन्ध्यां दिवसनिशयोरन्तरचरीम् ॥

ahaḥ sūte savyaṃ tava nayanamarkātmakatayā
triyāmāṃ vāmaṃ te sṛjati rajanīnāyakatayā

tṛtīyā te dṛṣṭirdaradalitahemāmbujaruciḥ
samādhatte sandhyāṃ divasaniśayorantaracarīm

48.

Sunlike,
your right eye
births the day

Moonlike,
your left eye creates
tripartite night

Like a just-burst
golden lotus, your
third eye

places twilight
precisely

between day and night

49.

विशाला कल्याणी स्फुटरुचिरयोध्या कुवलयैः
कृपाधाराधारा किमपि मधुराभोगवतिका ।

अवन्ती दृष्टिस्ते बहुनगरविस्तारविजया
ध्रुवं तत्तन्नामव्यवहरणयोग्या विजयते ॥

viśālā kalyāṇī sphuṭarucirayodhyā kuvalayaiḥ
kṛpādhārādhārā kimapi madhurābhogavatikā

avantī dṛṣṭiste bahunagaravistāravijayā
dhruvaṃ tattannāmavyavaharaṇayogyā vijayate

49.[*]

Your glance prevails

its attributes
like each of these names
(of cities)

Vast Viśālā
Auspicious Kalyāṇī

Inimitable even by blue
lotus blossoms
Ayodhyā

Flow of compassion
Dhārā

Indescribably sweet
Madhurā

Revelling Bhogavati
Protective Avantī

Victorious Vijayā
encompassing many cities

50.

कवीनां संदर्भस्तबकमकरन्दैकरसिकं
कटाक्षव्याक्षेपभ्रमरकलभौ कर्णयुगलम् ।

अमुञ्चन्तौ दृष्ट्वा तव नवरसास्वादतरला-
वसूयासंसर्गादलिकनयनं किञ्चिदरुणम् ॥

kavīnāṃ saṃdarbhastabakamakarandaikarasikaṃ
kaṭākṣavyākṣepabhramarakalabhau karṇayugalam

amuñcantau dṛṣṭvā tava navarasāsvādataralā-
vasūyāsaṃsargādalikanayanaṃ kiñcidaruṇam

50.

Seeing your eyes
slide sidelong

like a pair of distracted
young bees

that can't let go the nectar
of bouquets

that your ears are intent
to taste

—poet's paeans
of nine delectable rasas—

your third eye goes red
from a burst of envy

51.

शिवे श्रृङ्गारार्द्रा तदितरजने कुत्सनपरा
सरोषा गङ्गायां गिरिशचरिते विस्मयवती ।

हराहिभ्यो भीता सरसिरुहसौभाग्यजयिनी
सखीषु स्मेरा ते मयि जननि दृष्टिः सकरुणा ॥

śive śṛṅgārārdrā taditarajane kutsanaparā
saroṣā gaṅgāyāṁ giriśacarite vismayavatī

harāhibhyo bhītā sarasiruhasaubhāgyajayinī
sakhīṣu smerā te mayi janani dṛṣṭiḥ sakaruṇā

51.*

O Mother,
your glance—

Passionate, tender, when
you look at Śiva

At others,
contemptuous

In fury when you
see Gaṅgā

Amazed by the chronicles
of Śiva's adventures

Jittery from Śiva's
snakes

Eyes a heroic red
like the hue of lotuses

At women friends,
all smiles

Compassionate
towards me

52.

गते कर्णाभ्यर्णं गरुत इव पक्ष्माणि दधती
पुरां भेत्तुश्चित्तप्रशमरसविद्रावणफले ।

इमे नेत्रे गोत्राधरपतिकुलोत्तंसकलिके
तवाकर्णाकृष्टस्मरशरविलासं कलयतः ॥

gate karṇābhyarṇaṃ garuta iva pakṣmāṇi dadhatī
purām bhettuścittapraśamarasavidrāvaṇaphale

ime netre gotrādharapatikulottaṃsakalike
tavākarṇākṛṣṭasmaraśaravilāsaṃ kalayataḥ

52.

O flower bud

Crowning glory of
the lineage of Himavān,
lord of mountains

These eyes elongated
to the ears

with feathery lashes
resemble

Kāma’s arrow drawn
up to the ear

These eyes disturb
the peace of mind

of Śiva, destroyer
of Pura

53.

विभक्तत्रैवर्ण्यं व्यतिकरितलीलाञ्जनतया
विभाति त्वन्नेत्रत्रितयमिदमीशानदयिते ।

पुनः स्रष्टुं देवान् द्रुहिणहरिरुद्रानुपरतान्
रजः सत्त्वं बिभ्रत्तम इति गुणानां त्रयमिव ॥

vibhaktatraivarṇyaṃ vyatikaritalīlāñjanatayā
vibhāti tvannetratritayamidamīśānadayite

punaḥ sraṣṭuṃ devān druhiṇaharirudrānuparatān
rajaḥ sattvaṃ bibhrattama iti guṇānāṃ trayamiva

53.*

O beloved of Śiva

Bluish eyeshadow makes
your three eyes shine

with three particular
colours

like three qualities
sattva, rajas and tamas

as if to recreate the trinity
Brahmā, Viṣṇu and Rudra

when they have ceased
at the end of the world

54.

पवित्रीकर्तुं नः पशुपतिपराधीनहृदये
दयामित्रैर्नेत्रैररुणधवलश्यामरुचिभिः ।

नदः शोणो गङ्गा तपनतनयेति ध्रुवममुं
त्रयाणां तीर्थानामुपनयसि सम्भेदमनघम् ॥

pavitrīkartuṃ naḥ paśupatiparādhīnahṛdaye
dayāmitrairnetrairaruṇadhavalaśyāmarucibhiḥ

nadaḥ śoṇo gaṅgā tapanatanayeti dhruvamamuṃ
trayāṇāṃ tīrthānāmupanayasi sambhedamanagham

54.

O whose heart
is lost to Śiva

To purify us, your
compassionate eyes

red, white and dusky (like)
the rivers Śoṇa, Gaṅgā

and the sun's daughter
Yamunā

transport us for sure
to the sinless

confluence of these three
pilgrimage spots

55.

निमेषोन्मेषाभ्यां प्रलयमुदयं याति जगती
तवेत्याहुः सन्तो धरणिधरराजन्यतनये ।

त्वदुन्मेषाज्जातं जगदिदमशेषं प्रलयतः
परित्रातुं शङ्के परिहृतनिमेषास्तव दृशः ॥

nimeṣonmeṣābhyāṁ pralayamudayaṁ yāti jagatī
tavetyāhuḥ santo dharaṇidhararājanyatanaye

tvadunmeṣājjātaṁ jagadidamaśeṣaṁ pralayataḥ
paritrātuṁ śaṅke parihṛtanimeṣāstava dṛśaḥ

55.

O daughter of
the king of mountains

Sages say the world ends
and begins

with the closing and opening
of your eyes

but I suspect

your eyes gave up
blinking

to save this whole world
from annihilation

this world that was created
by opening your eyes

56.

तवापर्णे कर्णेजपनयनपैशुन्यचकिता
निलीयन्ते तोये नियतमनिमेषाः शफरिकाः ।

इयं च श्रीर्बद्धच्छदपुटकवाटं कुवलयम्
जहाति प्रत्यूषे निशि च विघटय्य प्रविशति ॥

tavāparṇe karṇejapanayanapaiśunyacakitā
nilīyante toye niyatamanimeṣāḥ śapharikāḥ

iyaṃ ca śrīrbaddhacchadapuṭakavāṭaṃ kuvalayaṃ
jahāti pratyūṣe niśi ca vighaṭayya praviśati

56.*

O eternal one,

the female śafarikā fish
sure hide in the water

without a wink
scared

that your eyes
tell tales to your ears

As for Beauty,
she leaves

the folded enclosure
of blue lily petals

at daybreak (the moment
you open your eyes)

enters abruptly
only at night

57.

दृशा द्राघीयस्या दरदलितनीलोत्पलरुचा
दवीयांसं दीनं स्नपय कृपया मामपि शिवे ।

अनेनायं धन्यो भवति न च ते हानिरियता
वने वा हर्म्ये वा समकरनिपातो हिमकरः ॥

dṛśā drāghīyasyā daradalitanīlotpalarucā
davīyāṃsaṃ dīnaṃ snapaya kṛpayā māmapi śive

anenāyaṃ dhanyo bhavati na ca te hāniriyatā
vane vā harmye vā samakaranipāto himakaraḥ

57.

O Śiva's consort

Please let the glance
from your long eyes

lovely like just-burst
blue lotuses

also fall on
poor me, so distant

as a moonbeam
falls equally

on both palace
and jungle

Then this (devotee) is blessed
and no harm to you either

58.

अरालं ते पालीयुगलमगराजन्यतनये
न केषामाधत्ते कुसुमशरकोदण्डकुतुकम् ।

तिरश्चीनो यत्र श्रवणपथमुल्लङ्घ्य विलस-
न्नपाङ्गव्यासङ्गो दिशति शरसन्धानधिषणाम् ॥

arālaṃ te pālīyugalamagarājanyatanaye
na keṣāmādhatte kusumaśarakodaṇḍakutukam

tiraścīno yatra śravaṇapathamullaṅghya vilasann-
apāṅgavyāsaṅgo diśati śarasandhānadhiṣaṇām

58.

Who does not recall

the flower arrow
and bow (of Kāma)

looking at your slanting
cheekbones

O daughter of
the king of mountains

your sidelong glance
sparkling above the ear line

suggests an arrow
fixed to a bow

59.

स्फुरद्गण्डाभोगप्रतिफलितताटङ्कयुगलं
चतुश्चक्रं मन्ये तव मुखमिदं मन्मथरथम् ।

यमारुह्य द्रुह्यत्यवनिरथमर्केन्दुचरणं
महावीरो मारः प्रमथपतये सज्जितवते ॥

sphuradgaṇḍābhogapratiphalitatāṭaṅkayugalaṃ
catuścakraṃ manye tava mukhamidaṃ manmatharatham

yamāruhya druhyatyavanirathamarkenducaraṇaṃ
mahāvīro māraḥ pramathapataye sajjitavate

59.[*]

A pair of earrings reflect
in your glowing cheeks

I believe your face is
the four-wheeled

chariot of Kāma

Climbing it
the great hero Kāma

plotted to fight Śiva
the lord of Pramathas

whose chariot is the earth
sun and moon, its wheels

60.

सरस्वत्याः सूक्तीरमृतलहरीकौशलहरीः
पिबन्त्याः शर्वाणि श्रवणचुलुकाभ्यामविरलम् ।

चमत्कारश्लाघाचलितशिरसः कुण्डलगणो
झणत्कारैस्तारैः प्रतिवचनमाचष्ट इव ते ॥

sarasvatyāḥ sūktīramṛtalaharīkauśalaharīḥ
pibantyāḥ śarvāṇi śravaṇaculukābhyāmaviralam

camatkāraślāghācalitaśirasaḥ kuṇḍalagaṇo
jhaṇatkāraistāraiḥ prativacanamācaṣṭa iva te

60.*

O Śiva's spouse

You drink with your ears
as with cupped hands

without pause

the wise words
of goddess Sarasvatī

that surpass the effects
of waves of nectar

When you nod
in wonder and praise

your earrings tinkle
loudly

as if echoing
agreement

61.

असौ नासावंशस्तुहिनगिरिवंशध्वजपटि
त्वदीयो नेदीयः फलतु फलमस्माकमुचितम् ।

वहत्यन्तर्मुक्ताः शिशिरकरनिश्वासगलितं
समृद्ध्या यत्तासां बहिरपि च मुक्तामणिधरः ॥

asau nāsāvaṃśastuhinagirivaṃśadhvajapaṭi
tvadīyo nedīyaḥ phalatu phalamasmākamucitam

vahatyantarmuktāḥ śiśirakaraniśvāsagalitaṃ
samṛddhyā yattāsāṃ bahirapi ca muktāmaṇidharaḥ

61.*

O banner on the rod
of snow mountain's lineage

May your bamboo-like
nose ridge soon give

the fruit of apt
rewards

It carries pearl drops within
sculpted by cool breath

so plentiful
even the outside

wears a pearl

62.

प्रकृत्या रक्तायास्तव सुदति दन्तच्छदरुचेः
प्रवक्ष्ये सादृश्यं जनयतु फलं विद्रुमलता ।

न बिम्बं तद्बिम्बप्रतिफलनरागादरुणितं
तुलामध्यारोढुं कथमिव विलज्जेत कलया ॥

prakṛtyā raktāyāstava sudati dantacchadaruceḥ
pravakṣye sādṛśyaṃ janayatu phalaṃ vidrumalatā

na bimbaṃ tadbimbapratiphalanarāgādaruṇitaṃ
tulāmadhyāroḍhuṃ kathamiva vilajjeta kalayā

62.*

O goddess with pretty teeth
I will say

what compares to your
naturally red lips

Let the (red) coral vine
bear fruit

No, not the bimba fruit

that just reflects
your ruddy lips

Put up front for even
the slightest comparison

will it not be very
embarrassed

63.

स्मितज्योत्स्नाजालं तव वदनचन्द्रस्य पिबतां
चकोराणामासीदतिरसतया चञ्चुजडिमा ।

अतस्ते शीतांशोरमृतलहरीमाम्लरुचयः
पिबन्ति स्वच्छन्दं निशि निशि भृशं काञ्जिकधिया ॥

smitajyotsnājālaṃ tava vadanacandrasya pibatāṃ
cakorāṇāmāsīdatirasatayā cañcujaḍimā

ataste śītāṃśoramṛtalaharīmāmlarucayaḥ
pibanti svacchandaṃ niśi niśi bhṛśaṃ kāñjikadhiyā

63.[*]

Too sweet

Drinking
the expansive net of light

from your moon face

the beaks of cakora birds
went insensate

So now, night after night
they drink

waves of nectar
of cool moon rays

like sour starch
as much as they wish

64.

अविश्रान्तं पत्युर्गुणगणकथाम्रेडनजपा
जपापुष्पच्छाया तव जननि जिह्वा जयति सा ।

यदग्रासीनायाः स्फटिकदृषदच्छच्छविमयी
सरस्वत्या मूर्तिः परिणमति माणिक्यवपुषा ॥

aviśrāntaṃ patyurguṇagaṇakathāmreḍanajapā
japāpuṣpacchāyā tava janani jihvā jayati sā

yadagrāsīnāyāḥ sphaṭikadṛṣadacchacchavimayī
sarasvatyā mūrtiḥ pariṇamati māṇikyavapuṣā

64.

O Mother

Untiringly repeating
the many legends

of your husband's exploits

your red tongue
surpasses the hibiscus

the flower of japa
(of repetitive chants)

It's so ruddy

the crystal clear
complexion of Sarasvatī

seated at the tip
of your tongue

transforms to a
ruby-red hue

65.

रणे जित्वा दैत्यानपहृतशिरस्त्रैः कवचिभिर्-
निवृत्तैश्चण्डांशत्रिपुरहरनिर्माल्यविमुखैः ।

विशाखेन्द्रोपेन्द्रैः शशिविशदकर्पूरशकला
विलीयन्ते मातस्तव वदनताम्बूलकबलाः ॥

raṇe jitvā daityānapahṛtaśirastraiḥ kavacibhir-
nivṛttaiścaṇḍāṃśatripuraharanirmālyavimukhaiḥ

viśākhendropendraiḥ śaśiviśadakarpūraśakalā
vilīyante mātastava vadanatāmbūlakabalāḥ

65.

Back after victory
in war with demons

helmets off
but still in armour

Kumāra, son of Śiva-Pārvatī
Indra, chief of the gods
Viṣṇu, creator

reject Śiva's leftovers—
Caṇḍa's share

to relish the chewed betel
and moon-white

flakes of camphor
spat from your mouth

66.

विपञ्चा गायन्ती विविधमपदानं पशुपतेः
त्वयारब्धे वक्तुं चलितशिरसा साधुवचने ।

तदीयैर्माधुर्यैरपलपिततन्त्रीकलरवां
निजां वीणां वाणी निचुलयति चोलेन निभृतम् ॥

vipañcyā gāyantī vividhamapadānaṃ paśupateḥ
tvayārabdhe vaktuṃ calitaśirasā sādhuvacane

tadīyairmādhuryairapalapitatantrīkalaravāṃ
nijāṃ vīṇāṃ vāṇī niculayati colena nibhṛtam

66.

When Sarasvatī sings
with her vīṇā

of the many glories
of Śiva

as you begin to nod
your head

say appreciative
words

the melody of her instrument
is outdone

by your sweetness

She puts away her own vīṇā
quietly

in its case

67.

करग्रेण स्पृष्टं तुहिनगिरिणा वत्सलतया
गिरीशेनोदस्तं मुहुरधरपानाकुलतया ।

करग्राह्यं शम्भोर्मुखमुकुरवृन्तं गिरिसुते
कथङ्कारं ब्रूमस्तव चुबुकमौपम्यरहितम् ॥

karāgreṇa spṛṣṭaṃ tuhinagiriṇā vatsalatayā
girīśenodastaṃ muhuradharapānākulatayā

karagrāhyaṃ śambhormukhamukuravṛntaṃ girisute
kathaṅkāraṃ brūmastava cubukamaupamyarahitam

67.

O daughter of the mountain

How can we describe
your chin

so incomparable

touched fondly by
the fingers of

snow mountain (your
father)

Raised again and again

by the lord of mountains (Śiva),
intent to sip your lips

The handle of a mirror
to Śiva's face

fit to be grasped by Śiva

68.

भुजाश्लेषान् नित्यं पुरदमयितुः कण्टकवती
तव ग्रीवा धत्ते मुखकमलनालश्रियमियम् ।

स्वतः श्वेता कालागुरुबहुलजम्बालमलिना
मृणालीलालित्यं वहति यदधो हारलतिका ॥

bhujāśleṣān nityaṃ puradamayituḥ kaṇṭakavatī
tava grīvā dhatte mukhakamalanālaśriyamiyam

svataḥ śvetā kālāgurubahulajambālamalinā
mṛṇālīlālityaṃ vahati yadadho hāralatikā

68.

Constantly horripilated
from the embrace

of the arms of
the vanquisher of cities, Śiva

your neck

has the beauty of
a stalk to your lotus face

Below it

a string of pearls
fair in itself, but

darkened by ample
herbal agaru paste

lovely as the soft fibrous
roots on a lotus stem

69.

गले रेखास्तिस्रो गतिगमकगीतैकनिपुणे
विवाहव्यानद्धप्रगुणगुणसङ्ख्याप्रतिभुवः ।

विराजन्ते नानाविधमधुररागाकरभुवां
त्रयाणां ग्रामाणां स्थितिनियमसीमान इव ते ॥

gale rekhāstisro gatigamakagītaikanipuṇe
vivāhavyānaddhapraguṇaguṇasaṅkhyāpratibhuvaḥ

virājante nānāvidhamadhurarāgākarabhuvāṃ
trayāṇāṃ grāmāṇāṃ sthitiniyamasīmāna iva te

69.*

O sole expert

in manner, modulation
and song

Three creases
at your neck—

they shine
on par

with three
wedding threads

like the outer limits
of three

fundamental scales
in music

sources of many various
melodious

musical formulas

70.

मृणालीमृद्वीनां तव भुजलतानां चतसृणां
चतुर्भिः सौन्दर्यं सरसिजभवः स्तौति वदनैः ।

नखेभ्यः सन्त्रस्यन् प्रथममथनादन्धकरिपो-
श्चतुर्णां शीर्षाणां सममभयहस्तार्पणधिया ॥

mṛṇālīmṛdvīnāṃ tava bhujalatānāṃ catasṛṇāṃ
caturbhiḥ saundaryaṃ sarasijabhavaḥ stauti vadanaiḥ

nakhebhyaḥ santrasyan prathamamathanādandhakaripoś-
caturṇāṃ śīrṣāṇāṃ samamabhayahastārpaṇadhiyā

70.*

Your four arms

vine-like, soft
as lotus stalks

Lotus-born Brahmā
praises their beauty

with his four faces

Terrified of the nails
of Andhaka's foe Śiva

from what happened
before

he hopes for a sign from you
a mystic sign, mudrā

of fearlessness and protection
for his four heads

71.

नखानामुद्द्योतैर्नवनलिनरागं विहसतां
कराणां ते कान्तिं कथय कथयामः कथमुमे ।

कयाचिद्वा साम्यं भजतु कलया हन्त कमलं
यदि क्रीडल्लक्ष्मीचरणतललाक्षारसचणम् ॥

nakhānāmudyotairnavanalinarāgaṃ vihasatāṃ
karāṇāṃ te kāntiṃ kathaya kathayāmaḥ kathamume

kayācidvā sāmyaṃ bhajatu kalayā hanta kamalaṃ
yadi krīḍallakṣmīcaraṇatalalākṣārasacaṇam

71.

Do tell, how do
we describe

the radiance of
your hands

lit by your
fingernails

that mocks
morning lotuses

By chance the lotus
may share

a faint resemblance
from the lac on the soles

of the feet of dancing
goddess Lakṣmī

72.

समं देवि स्कन्दद्विपवदनपीतं स्तनयुगं
तवेदं नः खेदं हरतु सततं प्रस्नुतमुखम् ।

यदालोक्याशङ्काकुलितहृदयो हासजनकः
स्वकुम्भौ हेरम्बः परिमृशति हस्तेन झटिति ॥

samaṃ devi skandadvipavadanapītaṃ stanayugaṃ
tavedaṃ naḥ khedaṃ haratu satataṃ prasnutamukham

yadālokyāśaṅkākulitahṛdayo hāsajanakaḥ
svakumbhau herambaḥ parimṛśati hastena jhaṭiti

72.

O Goddess

Nipples always
exuding milk

your breasts suckled
at the same time

by Kumāra and
elephant-headed Gaṇeśa

May contemplating this
take away our sorrows

Looking on, bewildered
Gaṇeśa suddenly

touches his own lobes
with his trunk—

—funny

73.

अमू ते वक्षोजावमृतरसमाणिक्यकुतुपौ
न सन्देहस्पन्दो नगपतिपताके मनसि नः ।

पिबन्तौ तौ यस्मादविदितवधूसङ्गरसिकौ
कुमारावद्यापि द्विरदवदनक्रौञ्चदलनौ ॥

amū te vakṣojāvamṛtarasamāṇikyakutupau
na sandehaspando nagapatipatāke manasi naḥ

pibantau tau yasmādaviditavadhūsaṅgarasikau
kumārāvadyāpi dviradavadanakrauñcadalanau

73.*

O banner of the lord
of the mountain

These, your breasts,
are nectar-filled ruby jars

We do not have even
the slightest tremor

of doubt in our mind

It is by feeding
at your breasts that

even today
elephant-headed Gaṇeśa

and Kārtikeya who split
the Krauñca mountain

are virgins
not having known

sexual pleasure
with women

74.

वहत्यम्ब स्तम्बेरमदनुजकुम्भप्रकृतिभिः
समारब्धां मुक्तामणिभिरमलां हारलतिकाम् ।

कुचाभोगो बिम्बाधररुचिभिरन्तः शबलितां
प्रतापव्यामिश्रां पुरदमयितुः कीर्तिमिव ते ॥

vahatyamba stamberamadanujakumbhaprakṛtibhiḥ
samārabdhāṃ muktāmaṇibhiramalāṃ hāralatikām

kucābhogo bimbādhararucibhirantaḥ śabalitāṃ
pratāpavyāmiśrāṃ puradamayituḥ kīrtimiva te

74.*

O Mother

At your chest
a string of flawless pearls

from the frontal lobe
of demonic-elephant
Gajāsura

dappled, reflecting
the bimba-fruit red

of your lips

Like the mixture of
ferocity and fame

of the crusher
of cities, Śiva

75.

तव स्तन्यं मन्ये धरणिधरकन्ये हृदयतः
पयःपारावारः परिवहति सारस्वतमिव ।

दयावत्या दत्तं द्रविडशिशुरास्वाद्य तव यत्
कवीनां प्रौढानामजनि कमनीयः कवयिता ॥

tava stanyaṃ manye dharaṇidharakanye hṛdayataḥ
payaḥpārāvāraḥ parivahati sārasvatamiva

dayāvatyā dattaṃ draviḍaśiśurāsvādya tava yat
kavīnāṃ prauḍhānāmajani kamanīyaḥ kavayitā

75.*

O daughter of the mountain

Your breast milk
given with kindness

I believe
from your very heart

Like the river Sarasvatī

flowing from the
ocean of milk

Relishing it
the draviḍa child became

the best composer
among the best

of poets

76.

हरक्रोधज्वालावलिभिरवलीढेन वपुषा
गभीरे ते नाभीसरसि कृतसङ्गो मनसिजः ।

समुत्तस्थौ तस्मादचलतनये धूमलतिका
जनस्तां जानीते तव जननि रोमावलिरिति ॥

harakrodhajvālāvalibhiravalīḍhena vapuṣā
gabhīre te nābhīsarasi kṛtasaṅgo manasijaḥ

samuttasthau tasmādacalatanaye dhūmalatikā
janastāṃ jānīte tava janani romāvaliriti

76.

O daughter of the mountain

Mind-born Kāma
body razed by

the line of fire
from Śiva's fury

sank into your
navel's deep pool

A streak of smoke
rose there

O Mother

people know it
as your line of hair

77.

यदेतत् कालिन्दीतनुतरतरङ्गाकृति शिवे
कृशे मध्ये किञ्चिज्जननि तव यद्भाति सुधियाम् ।

विमर्दादन्योऽन्यं कुचकलशयोरन्तरगतं
तनूभूतं व्योम प्रविशदिव नाभिं कुहरिणीम् ॥

yadetatkālindītanutarataraṅgākṛti śive
kṛśe madhye kiñcijjanani tava yadbhāti sudhiyām

vimardādanyo'nyaṃ kucakalaśayorantaragataṃ
tanūbhūtaṃ vyoma praviśadiva nābhiṃ kuhariṇīm

77.[*]

O consort of Śiva
O Mother

This (the line of hair),
at your slender waist

that shines
like a ripple of light

on the river Yamunā

seems to the wise
like ether

between your pitcher-breasts
that rub each other

squeezed, becoming
thin enough to

enter the navel-cave

78.

स्थिरो गङ्गावर्तः स्तनमुकुलरोमावलिलता-
कलावालं कुण्डं कुसुमशरतेजोहुतभुजः ।

रतेर्लीलागारं किमपि तव नाभिर्गिरिसुते
बिलद्वारं सिद्धेर्गिरिशनयनानां विजयते ॥

sthiro gaṅgāvartaḥ stanamukularomāvalilatā-
kalāvālaṃ kuṇḍaṃ kusumaśaratejohutabhujaḥ

raterlīlāgāraṃ kimapi tava nābhirgirisute
biladvāraṃ siddhergiriśanayanānāṃ vijayate

78.

O mountain's daughter

your navel's
something special

A still whirlpool
in river Gaṅgā

A water-trench for the vine
with two breast-buds

Fire-pit for the offering
of Kāma's prowess

House of pleasures
for Rati, his consort

Entrance to a cave
where Śiva's eyes

achieve
their yogic goals

79.

निसर्गक्षीणस्य स्तनतटभरेण क्लमजुषो
नमन्मूर्तेर्नारीतिलक शनकैस्त्रुट्यत इव ।

चिरं ते मध्यस्य त्रुटिततटिनीतीरतरुणा
समावस्थास्थेम्नो भवतु कुशलं शैलतनये ॥

nisargakṣīṇasya stanataṭabhareṇa klamajuṣo
namanmūrternārītilaka śanakaistruṭyata iva

ciraṃ te madhyasya truṭitataṭinītīrataruṇā
samāvasthāsthemno bhavatu kuśalaṃ śailatanaye

79.

O daughter of the mountain,
best among women

Your waist, already
slender by nature

stressed by the weight
of your breasts

looks bent as if
about to crack

steady as a tree
on an eroding riverbank

May your waist
always be well

80.

कुचौ सद्यःस्विद्यत्तटघटितकूर्पासभिदुरौ
कषन्तौ दोर्मूले कनककलशाभौ कलयता ।

तव त्रातुं भङ्गादलमिति वलग्नं तनुभुवा
त्रिधा नद्धं देवि त्रिवलि लवलीवल्लिभिरिव ॥

kucau sadyaḥ svidyattaṭaghaṭitakūrpāsabhidurau
kaṣantau dormūle kanakakalaśābhau kalayatā

tava trātuṃ bhaṅgādalamiti valagnaṃ tanubhuvā
tridhā naddhaṃ devi trivali lavalīvallibhiriva

80.*

O Devī

When your breasts
like two golden pitchers

suddenly perspire
rubbing at your armpits

your bodice tears
on the sides

'Enough of tearing'—

it is as if Kāma
tied the lavalī vine

three times
around your waist

to protect it

81.

गुरुत्वं विस्तारं क्षितिधरपतिः पार्वति निजा-
न्नितम्बादाच्छिद्य त्वयि हरणरूपेण निदधे ।

अतस्ते विस्तीर्णो गुरुरयमशेषां वसुमतीं
नितम्बप्राग्भारः स्थगयति लघुत्वं नयति च ॥

gurutvaṃ vistāraṃ kṣitidharapatiḥ pārvati nijān-
nitambādācchidya tvayi haraṇarūpeṇa nidadhe

ataste vistīrṇo gururayamaśeṣāṃ vasumatīṃ
nitambaprāgbhāraḥ sthagayati laghutvaṃ nayati ca

81.

O Pārvatī, your father

the lord of mountains
cut off his flanks

gave them to you
as dowry

That's why your
heavy hips flank

the entire earth
larger than it

making it lighter
by comparison

82.

करीन्द्राणां शुण्डान् कनककदलीकाण्डपटली-
मुभाभ्यामूरुभ्यामुभयमपि निर्जित्य भवति ।

सुवृत्ताभ्यां पत्युः प्रणतिकठिनाभ्यां गिरिसुते
विधिज्ञे जानुभ्यां विबुधकरिकुम्भद्वयमसि ॥

karīndrāṇāṃ śuṇḍān kanakakadalīkāṇḍapaṭalī-
mubhābhyāmūrubhyāmubhayamapi nirjitya bhavati

suvṛttābhyāṃ patyuḥ praṇatikaṭhinābhyāṃ girisute
vidhijñe jānubhyāṃ vibudhakarikumbhadvayamasi

82.

Both your thighs
surpass

the trunks of the best
of elephants

cluster of golden
plantain stems

O daughter of the mountain
O vedic savant

By repeatedly kneeling
to your spouse

your shapely hardened
knees surpass

the two frontal lobes
of Indra's elephant Airāvata

83.

पराजेतुं रुद्रं द्विगुणशरगर्भौ गिरिसुते
निषङ्गौ जङ्घे ते विषमविशिखो बाढमकृत ।

यदग्रे दृश्यन्ते दशशरफलाः पादयुगली-
नखाग्रच्छद्मानः सुरमकुटशाणैकनिशिताः ॥

parājetuṃ rudraṃ dviguṇaśaragarbhau girisute
niṣaṅgau jaṅghe te viṣamaviśikho bāḍhamakṛta

yadagre dṛśyante daśaśaraphalāḥ pādayugalī-
nakhāgracchadmānaḥ suramakuṭaśāṇaikaniśitāḥ

83.

O daughter of the mountain

To defeat Śiva

Kāma of five arrows
surely placed

twice the number of arrows
in your shin quivers

For at the tips of both feet

ten arrowheads
visible

as if your nails
filed

by the grindstone-crowns
of gods

84.

श्रुतीनां मूर्धानो दधति तव यौ शेखरतया
ममाप्येतौ मातः शिरसि दयया धेहि चरणौ ।

ययोः पाद्यं पाथः पशुपतिजटाजूटतटिनी
ययोर्लाक्षालक्ष्मीररुणहरिचूडामणिरुचिः ॥

śrutīnāṃ mūrdhāno dadhati tava yau śekharatayā
mamāpyetau mātaḥ śirasi dayayā dhehi caraṇau

yayoḥ pādyaṃ pāthaḥ paśupatijaṭājūṭataṭinī
yayorlākṣālakṣmīraruṇaharicūḍāmaṇiruciḥ

84.

O Mother
your feet

that the Upaniṣads wear
for a crown

that the river Gaṅgā
in Śiva's matted hair
washes

whose radiant red lac
is Viṣṇu's crimson
crest-jewel

Be so kind—
place them on my head too

85.

नमोवाकं ब्रूमो नयनरमणीयाय पदयो-
स्तवास्मै द्वन्द्वाय स्फुटरुचिरसालक्तकवते ।

असूयत्यत्यन्तं यदभिहननाय स्पृहयते
पशूनामीशानः प्रमदवनकङ्केलितरवे ॥

namovākaṃ brūmo nayanaramaṇīyāya padayos-
tavāsmai dvandvāya sphuṭarucirasālaktakavate

asūyatyatyantaṃ yadabhihananāya spṛhayate
paśūnāmīśānaḥ pramadavanakaṅkelitarave

85.[*]

Namaste, we say
to your two feet

pleasing to the eyes
with gleaming

wet red lac

When aśoka trees
in your pleasure garden

yearn to be
kicked by you

Śiva, lord of animals,
intensely jealous

86.

मृषा कृत्वा गोत्रस्खलनमथ वैलक्ष्यनमितं
ललाटे भर्तारं चरणकमले ताडयति ते ।

चिरादन्तःशल्यं दहनकृतमुन्मूलितवता
तुलाकोटिक्वाणैः किलिकिलितमीशानरिपुणा ॥

mṛṣā kṛtvā gotraskhalanamatha vailakṣyanamitaṃ
lalāṭe bhartāraṃ caraṇakamale tāḍayati te

cirādantaḥśalyaṃ dahanakṛtamunmūlitavatā
tulākoṭikvāṇaiḥ kilikilitamīśānaripuṇā

86.

Making a mistake,
faltering on your name

when he hung his head
embarrassed

you kicked your
husband's forehead

with your lotus feet

Peals of laughter
like your tinkling anklets

from Śiva's enemy
Kāma, who was razed,

rooting out
that longstanding thorn

(of resentment) within

87.

हिमानीहन्तव्यं हिमगिरिनिवासैकचतुरौ
निशायां निद्राणं निशि चरमभागे च विशदौ ।

वरं लक्ष्मीपात्रं श्रियमतिसृजन्तौ समयिनां
सरोजं त्वत्पादौ जननि जयतश्चित्रमिह किम् ॥

himānīhantavyaṃ himagirinivāsaikacaturau
niśāyāṃ nidrāṇaṃ niśi caramabhāge ca viśadau

varaṃ lakṣmīpātraṃ śriyamatisṛjantau samayināṃ
sarojaṃ tvatpādau janani jayataścitramiha kim

87.*

Your two feet
surpass the lotus

The lotus wilts
in snow

but they can tread
on a snow mountain

The lotus sleeps
at night

but they are radiant
all day and night

The lotus is a receptacle
for goddess Lakṣmī

They create prosperity
for Samaya devotees

O Mother
is that a surprise?

88.

पदं ते कीर्तीनां प्रपदमपदं देवि विपदां
कथं नीतं सद्भिः कठिनकमठीकर्परतुलाम् ।

कथं वा बाहुभ्यामुपयमनकाले पुरभिदा
यदादाय न्यस्तं दृषदि दयमानेन मनसा ॥

padaṃ te kīrtīnāṃ prapadamapadaṃ devi vipadāṃ
kathaṃ nītaṃ sadbhiḥ kaṭhinakamaṭhīkarparatulām

kathaṃ vā bāhubhyāmupayamanakāle purabhidā
yadādāya nyastaṃ dṛṣadi dayamānena manasā

88.

O Devī

The top of your feet

a hall of fame, where
misfortune has no place

How did wise poets
consider it hard

like the hardened shell
of a female tortoise

How did the kind-hearted
destroyer of cities, Śiva

place it
on a millstone

with his two hands
at the time of marriage

89.

नखैर्नाकस्त्रीणां करकमलसङ्कोचशशिभि-
स्तरूणां दिव्यानां हसत इव ते चण्डि चरणौ ।

फलानि स्वःस्थेभ्यः किसलयकराग्रेण ददतां
दरिद्रेभ्यो भद्रां श्रियमनिशमह्नाय ददतौ ॥

nakhairnākastrīṇāṃ karakamalasaṅkocaśaśibhis-
tarūṇāṃ divyānāṃ hasata iva te caṇḍi caraṇau

phalāni svaḥsthebhyaḥ kisalayakarāgreṇa dadatāṃ
daridrebhyo bhadrāṃ śriyamaniśamahnāya daḍatau

89.

O Caṇḍi

Your feet

that quickly grant
good things

to the poor
without stop

as if laugh

with their moonlike
toenails

at which celestial women
fold their lotus hands

as if laugh

at the celestial tree
whose fingerlike twigs

give fruit to those
already in heaven

90.

ददाने दीनेभ्यः श्रियमनिशमाशानुसदृशी-
ममन्दं सौन्दर्यप्रकरमकरन्दं विकिरति ।

तवास्मिन् मन्दारस्तबकसुभगे यातु चरणे
निमज्जन्मज्जीवः करणचरणः षट्चरणताम् ॥

dadāne dīnebhyaḥ śriyamaniśamāśānusadṛśī-
mamandaṃ saundaryaprakaramakarandaṃ vikirati

tavāsmin mandārastabakasubhage yātu caraṇe
nimajjanmajjīvaḥ karaṇacaraṇaḥ ṣaṭcaraṇatām

90.

Let my (six) senses be
a six-footed bee

immersed in
your feet

That grant the poor
the fortune

they hope for
at once

That exude
exuberant beauty

honey-heaps

charming as
hibiscus clusters

91.

पदन्यासक्रीडापरिचयमिवारब्धुमनसः
स्खलन्तस्ते खेलं भवनकलहंसा न जहति ।

अतस्तेषां शिक्षां सुभगमणिमञ्जीररणित-
च्छलादाचक्षाणं चरणकमलं चारुचरिते ॥

padanyāsakrīḍāparicayamivārabdhumanasaḥ
skhalantaste khelaṃ bhavanakalahaṃsā na jahati

atasteṣāṃ śikṣāṃ subhagamaṇimañjīraraṇita-
cchalādācakṣāṇaṃ caraṇakamalaṃ cārucarite

91.

O of graceful gait

Trying to learn
the way you move

the house swans
stumble but don't

quit the game

Your lotus feet

deliver the lesson
indirectly

with tinkling
gem-studded anklets

92.

गतास्ते मञ्चत्वं द्रुहिणहरिरुद्रेश्वरभृतः
शिवः स्वच्छच्छायाघटितकपटप्रच्छदपटः ।

त्वदीयानां भासां प्रतिफलनरागारुणतया
शरीरी श्रृङ्गारो रस इव दृशां दोग्धि कुतुकम् ॥

gatāste mañcatvaṃ druhiṇaharirudreśvarabhṛtaḥ
śivaḥ svacchacchāyāghaṭitakapaṭapracchadapaṭaḥ

tvadīyānāṃ bhāsāṃ pratiphalanarāgāruṇatayā
śarīrī śṛṅgāro rasa iva dṛśāṃ dogdhi kutukam

92.*

Attendants Brahmā, Viṣṇu,
Rudra and Īśvara

have become your
bedposts

Fair-complexioned
Sadāśiva

an apparent bedspread
white

Mirroring your hue
the red dawn

embodies the
erotic aesthetic (śṛṅgāra)

draws your pleasured
gaze

93.

अराला केशेषु प्रकृतिसरला मन्दहसिते
शिरीषाभा चित्ते दृषदुपलशोभा कुचतटे ।

भृशं तन्वी मध्ये पृथुरुरसिजारोहविषये
जगत्त्रातुं शम्भोर्जयति करुणा काचिदरुणा ॥

arālā keśeṣu prakṛtisaralā mandahasite
śirīṣābhā citte dṛṣadupalaśobhā kucataṭe

bhṛśaṃ tanvī madhye pṛthururasijārohaviṣaye
jagattrātuṃ śambhorjayati karuṇā kācidaruṇā

93.*

Hair's curly
Smile's slight

and by nature
straightforward

Mind, soft like
the siriśa flower

Nipples, hard
as grindstone

Slender at the waist

As for hips and
breasts, they

rise expansive

Compassionate
indescribable Aruṇā

Śiva's consort is
victorious

to protect the world

94.

कलङ्कः कस्तूरी रजनिकरबिम्बं जलमयं
कलाभिः कर्पूरैर्मरकतकरण्डं निबिडितम् ।

अतस्त्वद्भोगेन प्रतिदिनमिदं रिक्तकुहरं
विधिर्भूयो भूयो निबिडयति नूनं तव कृते ॥

kalaṅkaḥ kastūrī rajanikarabimbaṃ jalamayaṃ
kalābhiḥ karpūrairmarakatakaraṇḍaṃ nibiḍitam

atastvadbhogena pratidinamidaṃ riktakuharaṃ
vidhirbhūyo bhūyo nibiḍayati nūnaṃ tava kṛte

94.*

The mark on the moon
a dab of musk

The moon's watery orb
an emerald cup

filled with camphor bits
(moon digits)

so when you
use it daily

the hollow's depleted
(and the moon wanes)

It's true
again and again

Brahmā refills it
for your sake anew

(and the moon waxes)

95.

पुरारातेरन्तःपुरमसि ततस्त्वच्चरणयोः
सपर्यामर्यादा तरलकरणानामसुलभा ।

तथा ह्येते नीताः शतमखमुखाः सिद्धिमतुलां
तव द्वारोपान्तस्थितिभिरणिमाद्याभिरमराः ॥

purārāterantaḥpuramasi tatastvaccaraṇayoḥ
saparyāmaryādā taralakaraṇānāmasulabhā

tathā hyete nītāḥ śatamakhamukhāḥ siddhimatulām
tava dvāropāntasthitibhiraṇimādyābhiramarāḥ

95.*

You're the queen
of Śiva, destroyer of cities

Thus reverential homage
to your feet

inaccessible for those
with wavering senses

Thus immortals

led by Indra who
did a hundred sacrifices

attained incomparable powers
like aṇimā, the power

to become minute
by waiting at your door

96.

कलत्रं वैधात्रं कतिकति भजन्ते न कवयः
श्रियो देव्याः को वा न भवति पतिः कैरपि धनैः ।

महादेवं हित्वा तव सति सतीनामचरमे
कुचाभ्यामासङ्गः कुरवकतरोरप्यसुलभः ॥

kalatraṃ vaidhātraṃ katikati bhajante na kavayaḥ
śriyo devyāḥ ko vā na bhavati patiḥ kairapi dhanaiḥ

mahādevaṃ hitvā tava sati satīnāmacarame
kucābhyāmāsaṅgaḥ kuravakatarorapyasulabhaḥ

96.[*]

Is there a poet
who has not

enjoyed Brahmā's
wife Sarasvatī

With a bit of money
who isn't lord

of Lakṣmī

O faithful wife, first
among faithful wives

Other than Śiva, not
even the kuravaka tree

can attain your
bosom's embrace

97.

गिरामाहुर्देवीं द्रुहिणगृहिणीमागमविदो
हरेः पत्नीं पद्मां हरसहचरीमद्रितनयाम् ।

तुरीया कापि त्वं दुरधिगमनिःसीममहिमा
महामाया विश्वं भ्रमयसि परब्रह्ममहिषि ॥

girāmāhurdevīṃ druhiṇagṛhiṇīmāgamavido
hareḥ patnīṃ padmāṃ harasahacarīmadritanayām

turīyā kāpi tvaṃ duradhigamaniḥsīmamahimā
mahāmāyā viśvaṃ bhramayasi parabrahmamahiṣi

97.*

O partner of parabrahman
(the formless nameless ultimate)

Those who know
scriptures

call you Brahmā's wife
goddess of speech

Call you Viṣṇu's wife
Padma

Call you Śiva's consort
mountain's daughter

You are the indescribable
fourth

O Mahāmāyā (divine
power of illusion)

unfathomable, of
unlimited greatness

you make the world
go round

deluded

98.

कदा काले मातः कथय कलितालक्तकरसं
पिबेयं विद्यार्थी तव चरणनिर्णेजनजलम् ।

प्रकृत्या मूकानामपि च कविताकारणतया
कदा धत्ते वाणीमुखकमलताम्बूलरसताम् ॥

kadā kāle mātaḥ kathaya kalitālaktakarasaṃ
pibeyaṃ vidyārthī tava caraṇanirṇejanajalam

prakṛtyā mūkānāmapi ca kavitākāraṇatayā
kadā dhatte vāṇīmukhakamalatāmbūlarasatām

98.

O Mother, say when

may I, seeker
of knowledge

drink the lac-mixed water
that washed your feet

Like the juice of
chewed betel from

goddess Sarasvatī's
lotus mouth

that turns even
born mutes

into composers
of poetry

99.

सरस्वत्या लक्ष्म्या विधिहरिसपत्नो विहरते
रतेः पातिव्रत्यं शिथिलयति रम्येण वपुषा ।

चिरं जीवन्नेव क्षपितपशुपाशव्यतिकरः
परानन्दाभिख्यं रसयति रसं त्वद्भजनवान् ॥

sarasvatyā lakṣmyā vidhiharisapatno viharate
rateḥ pātivratyaṃ śithilayati ramyeṇa vapuṣā

ciraṃ jīvanneva kṣapitapaśupāśavyatikaraḥ
parānandābhikhyaṃ rasayati rasaṃ tvadbhajanavān

99.

Your devotee

a rival of Brahmā
and Viṣṇu

plays with Sarasvatī
and Lakṣmī

shakes the wifely
dedication of Rati

with his pleasing
body

immortal

destroys the bondage
of ignorance

enjoys the sweet sap
of ultimate bliss

100.

प्रदीपज्वालाभिर्दिवसकरनीराजनविधिः
सुधासूतेश्चन्द्रोपलजललवैरर्घ्यरचना ।

स्वकीयैरम्भोभिः सलिलनिधिसौहित्यकरणं
त्वदीयाभिर्वाग्भिस्तव जननि वाचां स्तुतिरियम् ॥

pradīpajvālābhirdivasakaranīrājanavidhiḥ
sudhāsūteścandropalajalalavairarghyaracanā

svakīyairambhobhiḥ salilanidhisauhityakaraṇaṃ
tvadīyābhirvāgbhistava janani vācāṃ stutiriyam

100.*

Like waving light to the sun
with the light of a flame
nīrājanaṃ

Like offering water from a moonstone
to the moon, source of nectar
arghyaṃ

Like trying to satiate the ocean
with its own water
tarpaṇaṃ

O Mother

These words of praise
Saundarya Laharī

are
your
words

NOTES

INTRODUCTION

1. There are specific rules for identifying guru and laghu syllables in Sanskrit prosody. A well-known mnemonic verse for this is: 'Sānusvāraśca dīrghaśca visargī ca gururbhavet. Varṇa saṃyogapūrvaśca tathāpādāntago'pi vā.' Laghu syllables include vowels a, i, u, ṛ, and ḷ. Guru syllables include vowels ā, ī, ū, ṝ, e, ai, o, au, 'anusvāra' ṁ, 'visarga' ḥ, any syllable followed by a conjunct consonant, and the final syllable in a line. Examples: two guru syllables—can-draḥ (moon), Kṛṣ-ṇaḥ (Kṛṣṇa, dark); three guru syllables—sva-bhā-vaṁ (nature).
2. W. Norman Brown (1958) lists all the manuscripts he referred to, and in conclusion, summarizes that there are 'two fairly well-defined recensions, a Northern, and a Dravidian (or Southern)' (p. 44).
3. See Rao (2019), pp. 88–93.

PART ONE: ĀNANDA LAHARĪ

VERSE 2

Sanskrit commentators note that this verse refers to Viṣṇu in the form of his serpent Adiśeṣa. In Indian mythology, Viṣṇu reclines on a many-headed serpent called Adiśeṣa, who also has the task of bearing the weight of the universe. Note, one thousand is like a placeholder for innumerable or just uncountable. It seems the poet of *Saundarya Laharī* is being jocular … Despite innumerable heads, it is not easy to carry the weighty speck of dust of Śakti's feet.

VERSE 3

Mihira-dvīpa-nagarī: Literally, sun-island-of town. According to Lakṣmīdhara, when the sun rises, it looks like it rises from an island town. Or—just as a sun overwhelms a stray little island town with light, Śakti dispels ignorance at once.

Cintāmaṇi: A legendary gemstone with mystical properties, believed to fulfil wishes and immediately take the possessor into a higher state.

Varāha: When the earth sank into the ocean, Viṣṇu incarnated as Varāha, the boar, dived in and retrieved the earth with his tusk.

Muraripu: Demon Mura was killed by Kṛṣṇa, or Viṣṇu, whose incarnation is Varāha.

VERSE 4

A mudrā is a natural sign, i.e., an expression of reality; thus, a smile is a mudrā of happiness. There are several mudrās in Indian aesthetics. Gods tend to be in postures of protective mudrās such as abhaya (be fearless) and varada (ready to grant a boon).

VERSE 5

On Viṣṇu becoming a woman: When the ocean is churned, out comes a pot of nectar (amṛta) that can confer immortality. To keep the demonic asuras away from this nectar, Viṣṇu takes on the form of an attractive woman called Mohinī and distributes the nectar in favour of the gods. In another story, Mohinī tricks the asura Bhasmāsura leading to his destruction.

Foe of the cities: Because Śiva destroyed the three cities of the asuras. For more on this, see note on verse 7.

VERSE 6

The gods need Śiva's help to kill the demon Tārakāsura, so they want him to come out of meditation and beget a son with Pārvatī. They send Kāma, the god of love, to disturb Śiva's meditation. Kāma's arrow finds its mark, and Śiva immediately feels attraction towards Pārvatī. But Śiva is furious that he has been disturbed, and opens his third eye, which annihilates Kāma. Śiva soon relents, and grants that Kāma can live, but he will be bodiless.

VERSE 7

Crusher of cities: These three cities belonged to the demons, and were on/ in earth, sky and heaven. Brahmā had granted a boon to some demonic devotees that these cities could only be destroyed by a single arrow. All the three cities are aligned during a particular astrological moment, and the gods are all ready with grand weaponry (earth as chariot, sun and moon as its wheels, Mt Meru as a bow, and the serpent Vāsuki as the bowstring). But Śiva demonstrates his calibre by destroying the cities without any weapons.

VERSE 9

This and the next verse describe the rise and passage of the kuṇḍalini along the seven cakras of the body. Cakras, depicted as funnel-shaped structures in the etheric sheath of our body, are the conduits of energy for our physical body. The awakening of different cakras is associated with the emergence of different abilities. For instance, the viśuddha cakra at the throat location is associated with the power of speech, and the ājñā cakra between the eyebrows is associated with inner vision. When dormant, kuṇḍalini Śakti remains coiled at the base of the spine. When awakened, Śakti rises along the arterial passage called 'suṣumnā nāḍī'. Piercing and activating the cakras, it reaches the crown of the head where it/she unites with the Śiva, who is consciousness. There is copious literature on this process in yoga and tantra.

VERSE 11

This verse describes the structure of the Śrīyantra, the aniconic form of Śakti. A Śiva triangle (Śrīkaṇṭa) points upwards, a Śakti triangle (Śivayuvati) points downwards. These nine triangles form the basis, and they are pierced or held by the centre (śambhu, or bindu). Moreover, they are encased by the lines of three circles with eight and sixteen petals. The verse notes forty-four, but the Śrīyantra has forty-three angles. The bindu may be counted as the forty-fourth angle.

VERSE 14

Treatises on yoga describe cakras as bright lotuses in specific hues, and the emanations of light from the cakras are described as rays or petals. The crown cakra has one thousand petals (sahasrāra, i.e., of one thousand). Here, the poet replaces that image with Śakti's feet.

VERSE 15

It is interesting to note that this verse is at odds with verse 4, where the poet declares that Śakti has no need for posturing with mudrās. Also, Śakti has four arms in this verse; in other depictions within *Saundarya Laharī*, she has eight arms.

VERSE 16

There are three different types of people in this verse: 'kavīndrāḥ', the best among poets; 'santaḥ', which I translate as 'wise' because they are a few; and 'satāḥ' (in 'satāṃ'), which I translate as 'truth-seekers' (just like in verse 15) because they care for profound words.

VERSE 17

The eight goddesses of speech are Vaśinī, Kameśvarī, Aruṇā, Vimalā, Jayinī, Modinī, Sarveśvarī and Kaulinī. Verses/mantras 15, 16 and 17 are believed to have the power to grant poetic talent.

VERSE 18

This and the next verse are believed to have the power to captivate women, and such a usage is called 'madana prayoga'.

VERSE 19

Commentators have interpreted Trilokī as a female personification of the cosmos, with the sun and the moon as her breasts.

'Yoni' means the female generative organ, or womb/source. 'The inverted triangle of yoni' refers to the upside-down triangular form.

VERSE 20

The 'sirā' or nerve/channel that exudes amṛta when activated is apparently in the head region. The other manuscript variants for sirayā mentioned by Kuppuswami (1976) are 'śirasā' (with the head) and 'rasayā' (by the rasa).

VERSE 21

The kuṇḍalini Śakti moves up the three spinal paths called iḍā, piṅgalā and suṣumnā, described as having the qualities of the sun, the moon and fire respectively.

VERSE 22

The verse plays on the double-entendre in the name 'Bhavānī', which is one of Śakti's names. 'Bhavāni' is the vocative singular form of Bhavānī, and as imperative verbal form of the root verb 'bhu', i.e., 'to be', it also means 'may I be'.

VERSE 23

Indian legends depict the figure of ardhanārīśvara as a composite of Śiva and Śakti, vertically divided—or shared—with Śakti on the left side and Śiva on the right. This verse imagines Śakti appropriating Śiva's side also, resulting in a peculiar blend.

VERSE 24

Commentators explain the figures of Brahmā, Viṣṇu, Rudra and Īśa as personifications of key functions during the universe's life cycle, and the process described here as 'tirodhāna' (disappearance). After the cycle of creation, preservation and destruction, everything is absorbed/dissolved into—and by—Īśvara or Īśa, who also then gets dissolved into Sadāśiva. Sadāśiva, the partner of Śakti, restores the process. This verse credits Śakti with the resurgence by noting that Sadāśiva gets his cue and command from a flick of Śakti's eyebrows.

VERSE 25

Everything in nature is made of three aspects or guṇas—sattva, rajas and tamas—which originate from Śakti.

VERSE 26

Brahmā's role is creation; it is said that he creates everything from five elements—earth, water, fire, air and ether. Viṣṇu's role is preservation, and it is a role without a pause. Yama is the god of death, and Kubera, the god of wealth.

The story about why Indra has a thousand eyes is anything but pretty. After Indra impersonates sage Gautama to be intimate with the sage's wife, he is cursed to have a thousand vaginas all over his body. Later, he obtains a reprieve from Brahmā, who turns the vaginas into eyes.

VERSE 28

When the gods and asuras churned the ocean to gain the nectar of immortality, among the initial substances that emerged was the suffocating poison hālāhala. Śiva saved the day by drinking this poison; because he held the poison in his throat, he is also called nīlakaṇṭha (blue-throat).

VERSE 29

Kaitabha is an asura who originated from Viṣṇu's earwax (along with the asura called Madhu), and went on to pester Brahmā. We find different narratives about how the duo were eventually killed, including in Devī Bhāgavata Purāṇa. As for Jambha, there are several asuras by this name. Jambha who was killed by Indra is mentioned in the Mahābhārata (Sabhā Parva, Chapter 98, Stanza 49). In Śrīmad Bhāgavatam (8.11.18), Jambha is an ally of King Bali and is beheaded by Indra's thunderbolt.

VERSE 31

The four goals (puruṣārtha) of human life are dharma (a moral way of life in tune with truth and justice), artha (wealth and other material assets), kāma (desires and emotional well-being) and mokṣa (spiritual progress, liberation).

VERSE 32

These fifteen syllables, when prefaced with the syllable 'śrīṁ' (the syllable that embodies Śakti), and initiated by a guru, form the sixteen-syllabic mantra called śodaṣākśarī.

VERSE 33

According to the tantric conventions, 'smara' (i.e., the name of the god of love) is a word/sound code for the mantra syllable 'klīṁ'; the word/sound 'yoni' (i.e., generative centre) is code for the mantra syllable 'hrīṁ'; and 'Lakṣmī' (well-being, goddess of fortune) is code for the mantra syllable 'śrīṁ'. Akṣavalaya could refer to a rosary used for mantra japa (repetition), or to the practice of repeating each letter of the alphabet along with the mantra. 'Surabhi' could mean fragrant, or could refer to Kāmadhenu, the wish-fulfilling cow.

VERSE 34

The nine traits of Śiva are kāla (time), kula (colours, lineage, Śrīcakra), nāman (names, nouns), jñāna (knowledge), citta (mind in its various forms), nāda (eternal sound and manifestations), bindu (dot, a source and gateway of creation), kalā (letters) and jīva (the one who enjoys, the being). Śakti's nine traits are the nine triangles, namely vāmī, jyeṣṭha, raudrī, ambikā, icchā, jñāna, kriyā, śāntā and parā. In the union of Śiva and Śakti, these nine traits are said to be 'samarasa' or similar, equal.

VERSE 36

Commentators explain that Śambhu refers to Paraśambhunātha, who along with Citparāmbā is the presiding deity of the ājñā cakra. The non-world is interpreted as the sahasrāra cakra, which is self-luminous and beyond the sun, moon and fire associated with the anāhata, ājñā and mūlādhāra cakras.

VERSE 38

Śiva and Śakti are the swan pair. This verse describes the contemplation of Śiva-Śakti in the heart cakra (anāhata), a location that is compared to a lake. According to legends, swans (haṃsas) can separate milk from water, drinking only the milk; the legend illustrates their ability to discriminate between what is, and is not, worthy. In the word/sound 'haṃsa', 'ha' stands for Śiva and 'sa' for Śakti. (Thus, the mantra 'haṃsa-sohaṃ'.) The eighteen sciences are the four vedas and six vedāṅgas (including śikṣā [phonetics], chandas [prosody], vyākaraṇa [grammar], nirukta [etymology], jyotiṣa [astrology] and kalpa [ritual sciences]), purva and uttara mīmāṃsā (vedic hermeneutics and non-dualism), nyāya (focuses on reasoning), purāṇas (ancient lore), dharmaśāstra (law and conduct), āyurveda (natural medicine), dhanurveda (archery), gāndharva śāstra (music) and nīti śastra (law).

VERSE 39

Śiva-Śakti are worshipped as Samvarteśvara and Samayāmbā, or Mahān and Mahatī, in the svādhiṣṭhāna cakra. *Saundarya Laharī* presents the svādhiṣṭhāna cakra as higher than the maṇipūra cakra; yoga treatises have it the other way around.

VERSE 40

As presiding deities of the maṇipūra cakra, Śiva and Śakti are called Taḍitvān and Taḍitvatī.

VERSE 41

Śiva and Śakti, due to their similarity or equivalence, are called 'Samaya' and 'Samayā' respectively. As presiding deities of the mūlādhāra cakra, they are called Nateśvara and Samayāmbā, or Mahānaṭeśvarā and Lāsyeśvarī.

PART TWO: SAUNDARYA LAHARĪ

VERSE 42

From verse 42 onwards, *Saundarya Laharī* begins to describe Śakti's physical form, from her crown to her soles.

VERSE 43

Vala is a demon and the brother of Vṛtra, who was also slain by Indra.

VERSE 44

Married women wear the vermilion mark in their hair parting (sindūra) as a sign of blessedness.

VERSE 45

Once, when the gods needed Śiva's help in killing the demon Tārakāsura, Śiva was deep in meditation. The gods dispatched Kāma, the god of love, to aim his arrows at Śiva. Kāma was successful, but Śiva was enraged at being disturbed and razed Kāma with his third eye.

VERSE 47

Kāma's arrows are flower-tipped, and the bowstring is made of bees. See verse 6.

VERSE 49

The double-entendre between names of cities in the Indian region and Śakti's glances has a backdrop in aesthetic convention. According to Indian aesthetic theory, each of these kinds of glances has distinct effects: Viśālā is an inward bloom that causes excitement; Kalyāṇī, which is an astonished glance, results in attraction; Ayodhyā, which is dilated, produces fear; Dhārā, a sluggish look, creates intoxication; the swirling glance Madhurā subjugates; the friendly look called Bhogavati hurts enemies; Avantī is an innocent look that causes enmity; and Vijayā is a half-closed look that causes death.

VERSE 51

This verse illustrates rasas, or aesthetic emotions, that Devī expresses depending upon whom or what she is responding to. In *Nāṭyaśāstra*, Bharata delineates eight rasas: śṛṅgāra (erotic), bībhatsa (disdain), raudra (anger), adbhuta (wonder), bhaya (fear), vīra (heroism), hāsya (mirth) and karuṇa (compassion). According to later convention (which is not without contention), there are nine rasas, including śānta (peace).

VERSE 53

Brahmā, Viṣṇu and Rudra dissolve into Śakti at the time of the annihilation of the universe.

VERSE 56

Blue lilies only bloom at night, and now we know why.

VERSE 59

I have not been able to decipher 'sajjitavate' to my satisfaction despite reading all the commentaries. Norman Brown takes a variant—'svaṃ jitavate'—for this word. I retain 'sajjitavate' because it is the version in Lakṣmīdhara's commentary, but I do not attempt a translation.

VERSE 60

Lakṣmīdhara interprets this verse as a description of Śakti's speech, and argues that Sarasvatī cannot possibly be speaking. The broader trend of ideas in the second part of *Saundarya Laharī* would support his point, for these verses describe Devī from head to toe. Some other commentators have argued that this verse describes Sarasvatī's speech based on a basic grammatical form—sarasvatyāḥ, i.e., Sarasvatī's. Moreover, I immediately recall the *Lalitāsahasranāmam* (614), which depicts Sarasvatī and Lakṣmī flanking Devī, fanning her.

VERSE 61

The breath inhaled along the left piṅgalā nāḍī is influenced by moon rays, hence the coolness. In Indian thought (ayurveda, yoga), there are three passages in our body (like arteries or nerves) for life-breath (prāṇa)—iḍā (to the right), piṅgalā (to the left), and suṣumnā (centre).

VERSE 62

The coral creeper is intense red in colour and does not bear fruit. Thus, the poet proposes the perfect impossible, and then turns to the next best option—bimba fruit. The *Lalitāsahasranāmam* (24) also describes Devī thus: 'nava-vidruma-bimbaśrī-nyakkāri-radana-cchadā'.

VERSE 63

Cakora birds are said to drink moon rays.

VERSE 69

The three scales are śadjam, mādhyamam and gāndhāram. According to *Sāmudrikālakṣaṇa*, a treatise that reads personality traits and prognostications from physical features, three lines are regarded auspicious in a woman.

VERSE 70

Andhaka is an asura whose story appears in several purāṇas. What happened before: There are several stories about how Brahmā is punished for some inappropriate act or the other. In the Brahmā-purāṇa, Brahmā sprouts extra heads so he can ogle Śatarūpa, a beautiful woman whom he created (thus, his daughter). When he sprouts a fifth head, he is literally cut back by Śiva for incestuous behaviour.

VERSE 73

When the demon Tārakāsura hid inside the mountain, Kārtikeya pierced it with his arrows.

VERSE 74

'Stamberama' means an elephant. The reference here is to a demon-elephant called Gajāsura who was vanquished by Śiva. Several commentators quote a proverb that says pearls originate in elephant skulls, bamboo stalks, clouds, snake hoods, seashells and sugarcane. Pearls found in elephant skulls are dappled in colour.

VERSE 75

The ocean of milk was churned for the nectar of immortality, and the river Sarasvatī is one of the treasures that emerged. Draviḍas are a race who populated the southern part of India. Who is this child who became the best among poets? Some commentators think that it refers to the Hindu seer Ādi Śaṅkarācārya himself; others are sceptical, wondering if he would have been so lacking in humility as to make such a big claim about himself. Yet others have speculated that the draviḍa child refers to Tirujñāna sambandhār (ca. seventh century CE).

VERSE 77

The water of the river Yamunā is considered dark, hence the comparison with the line of hair below Devī's navel.

VERSE 80

This verse offers an explanation for the three creases/folds on Devī's waist—very auspicious according to *Sāmudrikālakṣaṇa* (also see verse 69). The lavalī vine has a white hue, thus suggesting that Devī's waist folds have a sheen to them.

VERSE 85

Aśoka trees blossom when kicked by pious women.

VERSE 87

There are three styles of tantric practice: samaya, kaula and vāma. Samaya followers focus on internal worship.

VERSE 92

Also see verse 25.

VERSE 93

Whereas 'Aruṇā' means red-hued, commentators have explained it in this verse as a name for Śakti.

VERSE 94

The moon—Devī's cosmetic kit.

VERSE 95

In the first enclosure (āvaraṇa) of the Śrīcakra, the siddhis (extraordinary powers) are aṇimā, laghimā, mahimā, iśitva, vaśitva, prākāmya, bhukti, icchā, prāpti and sarvakāma.

VERSE 96

The kuravaka tree blossoms when embraced by a chaste woman.

VERSE 97

The fourth refers to turīya, the highest state of consciousness.

VERSE 100

Devī manifests as mātṛkās, or letters, from 'a' to 'kṣa'—therefore, whether syllables, words, mantras or all of language, it is all Devī.

REFERENCES

Avalon, Arthur. *Wave of Bliss, Ānandalaharī.* 4th Edition. Madras: Ganesh & Co., 1953.

Brown, W. Norman, ed. and trans. *Saundarya Laharī of Śaṅkarācārya*. Harvard Oriental Series, vol. 43. Cambridge, Massachusetts: Harvard University Press, 1958.

Kuppuswami, A. *Saundaryalaharī of Śrī Śaṅkara Bhagavatpādācārya*, with commentaries (in Sanskrit) Lakṣmīdhara, Saubāgyavardhanī, Aruṇāmodinī, Ānandagirīyā, Tātparyadīpinī, Padārthacandrikā, Ḍiṇḍima Bhāṣya, Gopālasundarī and Ānandalaharī Ṭīkā. Tiruchirapalli, India. 1976.

Rao, Mani. *Living Mantra: Mantra, Deity and Visionary Experience Today.* Cham, Switzerland: Palgrave Macmillan, 2019.

Sastri, Pandit S. Subrahmanya, and T.R. Srinivasa Ayyangar. *Saundarya-Laharī (The Ocean of Beauty).* Adyar, Madras: Theosophical Publishing House, 1965.

Subramanian, V.K. *Saundaryalaharī of Śaṅkarācārya.* Delhi: Motilal Banarsidass Publishers Pvt Ltd., 1977.

Tapasyananda, Swami. *Saundarya-Laharī of Sri Sankaracarya.* Madras: Ramakrishna Math, 1987.

ABOUT THE TRANSLATOR

MANI RAO is the author of ten poetry books, including *Sing to Me, New & Selected Poems*, *Ghostmasters* and *Echolocation.* Her books in translation from Sanskrit include *Bhagavad Gita* and *Kalidasa for the 21st Century Reader*. She did immersive fieldwork among tantric communities in Andhra–Telangana for *Living Mantra: Mantra, Deity and Visionary Experience Today.* Mani has an MFA in Creative Writing and a PhD in Religious Studies.